0000058281

10625

13.95
Bat
26460
1/4/82
9/82
2

17
HAM

WITHDRAWN

ST. ALBERT PUBLIC LIBRARY
31 FAIRVIEW BOULEVARD
ST. ALBERT, ALBERTA
T8N 3M5

AUCTION MADNESS

BOOKS BY CHARLES HAMILTON

Auction Madness (1981)
American Autographs (1981)
Great Forgers and Famous Fakes (1980)
The Signature of America (1979)
The Book of Autographs (1978)
Big Name Hunting (with Diane Hamilton, 1973)
Scribblers and Scoundrels (1968)
The Robot That Helped to Make a President (1965)
Lincoln in Photographs (with Lloyd Ostendorf, 1963)
Collecting Autographs and Manuscripts (1961)
Braddock's Defeat (1959)
Men of the Underworld (1952)
Cry of the Thunderbird (1950)

CHARLES HAMILTON

Auction Madness

AN UNCENSORED LOOK BEHIND
THE VELVET DRAPES OF THE
GREAT AUCTION HOUSES

ST. ALBERT PUBLIC LIBRARY
31 FAIRVIEW BOULEVARD
ST. ALBERT, ALBERTA
T8N 3M5

New York   EVEREST HOUSE   *Publishers*

Library of Congress Cataloging in Publication Data:

Hamilton, Charles, 1913–
   Auction madness

   Includes index.
   1. Auctions. I. Title.
   HF5476.H33   381'.1   81-12504
   ISBN: 0-89696-123-0   AACR2

Photographs used in this book are reprinted by permission of Sotheby Parke Bernet.

The excerpt on page 87 is reprinted from Great Forgers and Famous Fakes by Charles Hamilton. Copyright © 1980 by Charles Hamilton. By permission of Crown Publishers, Inc. The article on page 136 is Copyright © 1980 by The New York Times Company. Reprinted by permission. The illustration on page 196 is from Auctions and Auctioneering by Ralph Cassady, Jr. Copyright © 1967 by Ralph Cassady, Jr. Reprinted by permission of University of California Press. The article, "Washington Relic: $40,000 or $200?" is reprinted by permission of the New York Post. Copyright © 1976 by New York Post Corporation. The article by Guy Martin is used courtesy of Mr. Martin and The Soho Weekly News. Copyright © 1980 by The Soho Weekly News. Reprinted by permission.

Copyright © 1981 by Charles Hamilton
All Rights Reserved
Published simultaneously in Canada by
Beaverbooks, Don Mills, Ontario
Manufactured in the United States of America
designed by Judith Lerner
First Edition
RRD1081

To My Daughter

CYNTHIA CHAPIN HAMILTON

Acknowledgments

TO ALL OF THE following I am grateful for the use of photographs, or for reminiscences or for other help in the preparation of this book:

James Camner
Bruce Gimelson
Regina Reynolds
H. Keith Thompson, Jr.
Robert F. Batchelder
Charles W. Sachs
Seymour Halpern
Gary Grossman
Herman Darvick
Josephine Hughes
Dianne Gomez
Gretta Jacobson
Richard C. Schneider

Roselle S. Morse
Carol Mann
Jerry Gross
Sotheby Parke Bernet
Christie's
Plaza Art Galleries
The University of California at Los Angeles and at Berkeley
Nancy McGlashan
Herbert Melnick
Swann Galleries
Kenneth W. Rendell

But especially I am grateful to my daughter, Carolyn Brooks Hamilton, and my wife Diane Brooks Hamilton for reading large portions of the manuscript and offering many valuable suggestions.

Contents

AUCTION MADNESS

CHAPTER 1

Bidder's Fever:
The Incurable Disease

IT LACKED BUT two hours until auction time. Lusting collectors and dealers had crowded into my little gallery, quietly reconnoitering the lots about to be put on the block. A determined band, all of them, girding for the impending sale.

Standing with me was a tall, spare man with bright red hair. He put a bony finger on one of the lots, a sheet of paper bearing the huge, maniacal scrawl of Otto "Scarface" Skorzeny, notorious Nazi hit man and commando. "This is already mine," the thin man said savagely. "Do you understand? It's mine. Nobody else can have it."

At the sale there was a fierce battle for the Skorzeny document. From an opening bid of fifty dollars the offers rocketed madly as greedy speculators and wild-eyed collectors shouted or signaled their bids. When the tiny sheet was finally knocked down to the redheaded man for nine hundred dollars—more than ten times its actual value—his eyes glinted in triumph and the thrill of victory. As he rose to go into the hallway for a much needed cigarette, he whispered to me: "I told you it was mine."

Bidding at auction is the most exhilarating of all sports. It matures young men in a few seconds and instantly rejuvenates the moribund. It provides all the blood-pounding excitement of a real battle. And into the veins of even the most generous collector it injects the addictive drug of rabid greed.

Many times have I studied the covetous bidders who advance to the fray, buckled up in *aes triplex* (triple brass) and fortified against any overt act of kindness. They enter the salesroom nervously, moving their heads like automatons. They elevate their chins to sniff the prevailing winds. Who will be bidding on what? (All intended bids are top secret!) The combatants greet one another with jests that are not really funny or with words that are courteous but not cordial. They are ready for a ruthless struggle. As the crier mounts to the podium and the battle starts, their eyes narrow to slits of steel or else open wide in a deceptive blandness. Their jaws twitch and gradually come to a full clench. They are the Determined Ones. They are the greedy warriors who will compete for the plunder of man's past—the paintings, the precious relics, the glittering silver and gold, the letters and documents of the great.

What is really their motivation? Is it a love of beauty, a desire to preserve the cultural heritage of the world? Or is it a baser motive, something rooted in the dark corridors of the mind? Freud said the collecting mania was only a substitute for the sex drive. The object sought, he averred, is just a symbol of sexual love. His successors in the psychiatric business called the collecting urge a throwback to the oral and anal conditions of infancy, sucking and bowel control. Thus, say they, the acquisitive desire, strong in a magpie and even stronger in a human, is nothing more than a savage instinct, an uncontrollable desire to seize upon a treasure and hoard it away.

Certainly the miser does not admire the artistry of St. Gauden's beautiful design on the double eagle. Nor does his heart beat high for his country when he looks upon the head of liberty on the half eagle. He wants these handsome coins

only because they are gold that glitters, and to possess them
gives him a feeling of power.

Maybe the wild desire to win at auction goes back to
primeval days, when early man squirreled up food and fought
even to the death over whatever he considered to be of value.
It is human nature to pursue, to conquer, and to possess.
"Auction bidders are cannibals," said Bonaffe, a French
collector. "When closeted together, they devour each other."

Picture, if you will, the auction floor of the old Anderson
Galleries, long defunct precursor of Sotheby Parke Bernet.
There in the roaring twenties a few dozen dealers and a score
of collectors gathered weekly to wage war for paintings or rare
books. Dr. A. S. W. Rosenbach, the nabob of first editions,
used to show up fortified by ten fingers of Scotch and bid
furiously until every noteworthy prize fell to him. They
nicknamed him "Dr. R." and "Rosy," the second moniker
being not only an abbreviation of Rosenbach but a depiction
of the alcoholic flush on his cheek. Rosy won a mighty
reputation for besting all foes in the salesroom and sometimes, in his booze-inspired zeal, paid prices that put his
purchases for stock beyond the reach of even his most wealthy
and acquisitive clients. In short, the nabob got stuck with his
buys. But he never mended his ways. He lived in the grip of
auction madness. He had bidder's fever in its most malignant
form. And when he hated his competitor in the salesroom it
inspired him tenfold, and the fused motives of greed and hate
drove him to break all records for top prices.

For many, advanced bidder's fever compels them to bid on
a rare item merely because it is rare and others seek it, not
because it has intrinsic merit. If the bibliophiles who covet
Poe's *Tamerlane and Other Poems*, his rare first book now
valued at more than $100,000, were forced to read the
volume as a requisite to owning it, I doubt if the legendary
rarity would fetch more than a dollar or two on its next trip to

the block. My boyhood friend, Carl S. Dentzel, the late curator of the Northwest Museum in Southern California, was a true apostle of beauty, and many times I have watched him caress an old painting or a rare book as other men do a woman. But Carl invariably succumbed to greed. He bought anything and everything he thought others desired. Once he showed me a great stack of Remington paintings in one of his storage cottages. It never occurred to Carl to hang these beautiful paintings on his walls and enjoy them. He got his cultural kicks out of knowing that they were his and that they were safely squirreled away where no one else could ever get them.

Dr. Frank Siebert, perhaps the world's greatest expert on the North American Indians, often paid what I considered exhorbitant prices for unimportant pamphlets at public sales. He seemed to lose control of himself when he heard the cry of the auctioneer. It set his blood afire. He always tumbled for widely publicized rarities, and I once embarrassed him by stripping bare his motives.

"Why do you pay so much for early broadsides printed in little frontier towns?" I asked him, by way of casting out a bit of bait.

"Because they are the earliest printings, the definitive texts. They take us right to the source of the action, right where history is made."

"That's often not true," I said. "Suppose that the first printing, the definitive printing, let us say, of an account of an Indian massacre in Ohio were published in an ordinary New York newspaper of the time, a very common issue now worth about $10. Then, a few weeks later, somebody in Zanesville, Ohio, got the text from the New York paper and on a small press in Zanesville ran off about 50 flyers or broadsides describing the massacre, a printing of which only two or three copies survive. Would you not prefer the rare broadside, even though it was nothing more than a copy of the original publication? And even though you would have to pay a hundred times as much for it?"

Frank then admitted that he often sought items purely because of their rarity, not because of their value to scholars and historians.

Once in a while dealers and collectors battle for treasures out of sheer spite. Not long ago a prominent dealer came back from a sale in England with a handwritten letter of Shelley's for which he'd paid at least three times its value.

"Why did you pay so much for this Shelley letter?" I asked, while he was showing it to me.

"Merely to teach a lesson to a collector, a much needed lesson," he answered. "My Shelley customer thought he could bid without my advice and help and I simply would not permit it. I kept forcing him up until I ran him right through the ceiling and he had to drop out. In the future he will come to me when he wants a Shelley letter and let me bid for him."

The dream of every voracious huckster is an all-out "punching match," a bitter feud on the salesroom floor. Such good fortune overtook the auctioneer recently at the Skinner autograph sale in Boston late in 1980. Two inveterate collector-dealers, Dr. Maury Bromsen and Paul C. Richards, dueled savagely over desirable lots. The prices shot up in a dizzy spiral. Other would-be bidders watched in amazement as the two battled, each determined to carry away the gems of the sale. A neutral dealer, Mary A. Benjamin, was dismayed by the astronomic prices. The competition between Bromsen and Richards had reduced her to the status of a frustrated spectator. Finally she rose in anger and marched from the room.

Should you ever get caught in the no-man's-land of such a fierce skirmish, with the bids flying back and forth over your head, my suggestion is to follow the tactics of Mary A.

Benjamin and head for the trenches. Don't get drawn into the madness or you may wind up losing your wallet.

Bidder's fever is an infectious disease. If you sit next to a person who's got it you may catch it from him. When the fever flares up, you may pay too much for stuff you don't even want.

Once over a liquid lunch I asked the late Professor David A. Randall, famed curator of the Lilly collection at the University of Indiana Library, to tell me about his most memorable auction purchase.

"I'd had a few too many martinis," said Dave, "and while driving home I ran across a great concourse of cars parked along the road. I knew right away it was a country auction so I stopped to see the fun. It was pretty exciting, but the prices were very high, much too high to lure me. Cheap furniture and silverplate knocked down at double the retail worth!

"Still, the auction was exciting and I was eager to bid on something, anything. Just when I was about to give up and move on, the auctioneer's helpers carried out of the storage barn a huge moose head. A gigantic animal he must have been, for his great horns had a spread of about nine feet. Nobody would make a starting offer, so, half in jest, I pitched in a bid of fifty cents.

"'Sold!' cried the auctioneer. I left my name and address with an attendant and forgot the whole incident.

"About two weeks later on arriving home from work I saw, to my astonishment, a moose head on my front porch. It was so huge that its horn span occupied almost the entire length of the porch. It had not arrived alone. With it came a bill for cartage of $22.50, which my wife had paid."

"What did you do with the moose head?" I asked.

"I shelled out five dollars to have it hauled away. What else could I do? I couldn't move out of my home just to give it space, could I?"

Although bidder's fever is brought on mainly by avarice, there is an even more sinister cause of madness on the auction floor: I refer to the dealer, bidding for a client, who connives with the auctioneer or with a confederate to drive prices up far beyond their actual value, although sometimes there seems to be no explanation for high prices. In 1980 a Tsuchou vase, valued by some experts at about $25,000, was knocked down for $500,000 to an agent acting for the British Railway Pension Fund. Obviously the Fund has an enormous sum at its disposal and the directors of the Fund are intent upon investing this sum with as much dispatch as possible.

The ability to bilk one's clients at auction is a fine art, make no mistake about it. To succeed for a lifetime without detection or exposure, the auction-buying crook must have the cunning of a polecat, the ethics of a Gabon viper, and the acquisitive drive of a dung-beetle. All these feral qualities were uniquely fused in the late Lew David Feldman, a rare book and manuscript dealer who operated under a firm name devised from his cutely bastardized initials—The House of El Dieff. Feldman's consuming ambition, like that of several contemporary rare-book czars, was to dominate the auction world by his spectacular purchases and grandiose catalogs. In 1974 Lew published at a cost of $15,000 his Fortieth Anniversary catalog, a collection of forty rare and costly books and manuscripts. In a colophon he proudly announced the total buck value of the forty items ($1,925,077), a slip into bad taste that offended even his most vulgar competitors.

At times Feldman's adoration for money led him to take unnecessary risks, and once he lost a $200,000 gamble when he laid out this huge sum for an option on a precious Gutenberg Bible. Lew thought he had set the hook on a sucker but the sucker wriggled off and Lew forfeited his deposit, a loss that nearly gave him a coronary.

Feldman always thought and talked in terms of millions of

dollars. His oft-printed advertisement consisted of only one huge word, QVALITY. My wife Diane could never decide whether Lew intended this word to be pronounced with a Yiddish accent or merely hoped that it would give a classic flavor to his vulgarity by incorporating the Roman u.

Feldman's unwritten but always acted-upon philosophy was: "Knowledge and scholarship be damned. The buck's the thing. It's not what's in a rare book. It's how much you pay for it."

I'd often wondered why libraries employed as an agent this exquisitely tasteless man who limped about with Mark Twain's silver-headed cane and a supercilious sneer on his fat upper lip. Finally I asked an official at the New York Public Library why they gave their auction bids to Feldman.

"Lew can predict exactly what the lots we're interested in will fetch. He has a deep knowledge of rare books and manuscripts that enables him to forecast prices accurately in advance of the sale."

I mulled this answer over and concluded there is only one way anybody can foretell the future and that is by creating the future himself. You can predict the exact time of a man's death if you are the judge who sentences him to hang. Later I learned that Feldman sometimes connived to have his bids pushed up to his pre-sale predicted value. If the value of a Henry David Thoreau manuscript was estimated by the auction gallery at $2,000 and Feldman predicted it would fetch $8,000, he made certain that a secret bid to the auctioneer or from a confederate forced the selling price up to his predicted sum. This not only ensured the accuracy of his prognostication but quadrupled his commission.

The best deal Lew ever worked out was with the University of Texas where his "arrangement" with the chancellor, Harry Ransom, blew in a gusher for both men. They made millions by bilking the University Library. They bought virtually worthless collections privately, then sold them to the university at an immense profit. Lew cut the chancellor in for a percentage of the take and Ransom made sure that Lew's bills were quickly approved and promptly paid. Both men died rich, another proof of the old truism that crime pays.

The auction madness often hits a beginner and drives him berserk. He may act as if he's been bitten by a tarantula and wave his hands violently and even leap up and down. After the auction sale is over and he contemplates the wreckage he's wrought on his finances, he may go to the auctioneer and apologize: "I'm afraid I got a bit carried away and bought a few things I didn't intend to buy. What shall I do?"

Most auction houses will resell his purchases for him at a slightly lower cost than their usual commission, but since auction catalogs are prepared far in advance it may take six months before the rash bidder recoups.

At Sotheby Parke Bernet, a few years ago, a well-dressed young man, unknown to the galleries, bought heavily at an art sale, stocking up on rare and beautiful paintings. His purchases ran into hundreds of thousands of dollars. When the gallery presented its bill, he announced: "I'm broke. I have no money at all. Sue me if you wish. But it won't do you any good, because I haven't a bent kopeck to my name." The only recourse the gallery had was to resell at their own expense the paintings "purchased" by this man who had got so carried away by bidder's fever that he kept buying even though he knew he couldn't pay.

I once had a similar, but not quite so disastrous, experience. The angel that troubled my waters was a tottering old man who bid crazily and without restraint at one of my sales. When the auctioneer's hammer fell on the final lot, the old guy was the owner of more than $35,000 worth of manuscripts. He had snatched from my regular customers almost every single lot of importance.

"Don't worry about him," someone whispered to me. "He's good for it. Richer than Croesus."

It turned out that the old man was rich, very rich. He was on a terminal spending spree and had just blown tens of thousands on African art at the Hammer Galleries. But he was also pretty senile, only a brain cell away from being nuts. He'd escaped from the amiable custody of his family, found his way into my gallery, and gobbled up every historic and literary delicacy that appealed to him.

Several months later, when his bill was still unpaid, our vice president, H. Keith Thompson, Jr., traveled to the man's palatial home in Connecticut where he was confronted with a surly dog that guarded the huge iron gates. Keith finally eluded the hostile canine, got into the house, and collected several checks, installment payments that were all subsequently honored by the bank.

Six months later the guardians of the antediluvian victim of bidder's fever put his purchases up for sale at my auction. They got back every cent he'd spent and more, so maybe the old guy wasn't as crazy as we thought.

CHAPTER 2

The Elegant Hucksters

WHEN THE MAN from Christie's saunters down Park Avenue, ordinary folk turn and gape. His immaculate pin-striped trousers, neatly pressed morning coat, and deftly flaunted stick or umbrella all catch the eye. If he deigns to look about him, it is with an air of Olympian disdain. He appears to be a superior mortal of some sort, but he is, in fact, merely one of many identical snobs cloned from an elegant sire long put to pasture in the pages of Burke's Peerage. The Christie's man speaks no English, only British. And he is presumably an expert on something (and sometimes he is) but more often than not you will find him wanting.

This lack of knowledge explains why the Christie's man is got up as a gentleman. His attire is a substitute for learning. His British accent is designed to throw the Yankee yokels off guard and create the impression that behind this clipped lingo lurks a superior mind, a penetrating intellect, and an omniscient scholarship that would awe Erasmus.

Not a bit of it! If you are fooled by his garb and his gab, then you are fair game for the auctions that he and his associates conduct. You will cheerfully pay outlandish prices for the very "heirlooms" that your mother and grandmother pitched out in horror, hid in the attic, or retired to the basement.

Although the minions of Christie's and their fellow Britons, Sotheby Parke Bernet, outwardly take an indifferent view of money and speak of it with distaste, their entire organizations are as adroitly set up as any other huge conglomerate. Art and history, beauty and culture are merely products they package and sell.

As you observe the elegant huckster at work, haughtily crying the sale, apparently with utter disdain for the monetary sums that ratatat in snipped British from his lips, it is hard to realize that he is not always as much of an expert as he sounds.

And like many of the coxcombical criers he often looks upon his audiences with contempt. One huckster boasted: "I can get a crowd going so fast and furious that they'll bid on anything. I once tricked a woman into bidding on something she didn't even know about. And she loved it!" The elegant huckster's organization has, moreover, at last given up all pretense about being art lovers and purveyors and now has openly swapped its slogan of "fine art auctioneers" for a policy of selling anything that's worth a buck. The burgeoning conglomerates of Sotheby Parke Bernet and Christie's are adventuring into other and less romantic areas. Sotheby Parke Bernet has established a huge repair shop to transform busted-down antiquities into coveted treasures. Its expertise now includes real estate, boats, used cars, and even old houses. Its aristocratic experts can flush a toilet in a rundown mansion and tell you the state of the plumbing or peer up the exhaust pipe of an old Mercedes and give you a report on the carburetor.

There was a time when the auctioneers in the great galleries of America, in the glory days of Parke-Bernet, looked with warmth and affection on their merchandise. They understood books and autographs, furniture and china and paintings. They appreciated them and loved them and parted from their company with a measure of sorrow. Now

little is left of the great firm of Parke-Bernet and the men
with talent and knowledge who ran it. They were truly
merchants of beauty and culture. One of the last of these is
John Marion, talented son of Louis Marion, a towering figure
in the old Parke-Bernet. John is tall, good-looking, articu-
late, and ethical, rich in the ebullience of youth. He is and
always will be American in his outlook. Sotheby's will not
sack him from his post as president partly because he is good
at his job and partly because it dare not. Soon, of course, the
British firm must make the final break with American
tradition. It will jettison the names Parke and Bernet that
give the firm the despised American flavor.

One of Sotheby Parke Bernet's old customers complained
to me: "Sotheby Parke Bernet is like a massive machine.
Cold, impersonal, and with constant kinks that need attention. They've taken all the joy out of auctions."

As a philographer, I cannot witness the knocking down of
the letters of great authors at Sotheby Parke Bernet or
Christie's without recalling the poignant sonnet of Oscar
Wilde on the sale of Keats' letters. Unless you have brushed a
tear from your eye whilst perusing Keats' beautiful love letters
to Fanny Brawne you may not understand these lines, but if
you are a lover of Adonais you will read this sonnet with
sympathy:

> *These are the letters which Endymion wrote*
> *To one he loved in secret, and apart,*
> *And now the brawlers of the auction mart*
> *Bargain and bid for each poor blotted note.*
> *Ay! for each separate pulse of passion quote*
> *The latest price.—I think, they have not Art*
> *Who break the crystal of a poet's heart*
> *That small and sickly eyes may glare and gloat.*

Is it not said, that many years ago
In a far Eastern town some soldiers ran
With torches through the midnight, and began
To wrangle for mean raiment, and to throw
Dice for the garments of a wretched man,
Not knowing the God's wonder or his woe?

When Wilde wrote these lines, nearly a century ago, he was alluding to the commercial firms of Sotheby's and Christie's in London, then structured exclusively for dealers and to those purveyors of autographs who handled precious documents as other men deal in halibut and mackerel.

If you wander into Christie's and Sotheby Parke Bernet you will see many very attractive young girls whose neat appearance brightens the gallery. These are not, of course, ordinary young ladies. They have attended a special school for snobs. They are trained, most of them, in the art of the unseeing eye and the unhearing ear.

Do not be angry if they ignore or patronize you. This is part of their job. They are required to look and act superior, detached, and very cultured or they will be handed 78 quid or whatever and given their walking papers.

Sometime, when you are at liberty to observe, watch one of these well-schooled young ladies answer the phone. It is a study in aloof distaste. They handle the ugly, misshapen receiver with delicacy, almost as they would touch a rare Ming thing. They look straight ahead, with a dreamy, poetic detachment. Once in a while they may bang themselves in the lips with the unclean device because they are *too detached* from the menial mechanics of answering the phone. My friend, James Camner, who is an author and close observer of people, told me: "I watched a young woman at Sotheby's pick up a phone, delicately, all the while glancing about as if she were not really engaged in such a plebeian activity. She hit herself so hard on the teeth you could hear the crack clear across the reception room."

"And then?" I asked.

"Why, then," said Jim, "she smiled as if she'd done it on purpose."

I have noticed, lately, that the young ladies at Sotheby Parke Bernet are emulating the young ladies at Christie's. Snobbery is contagious. Should you arrive at Sotheby Parke Bernet before ten o'clock in the morning (the portals don't swing open until mid-matin) you will have to cool your O'Sullivans at the door. If the weather is clement, you can observe the superior young ladies, the clerical staff, carrying their tennis rackets ostentatiously as they float ethereally into the building. Their tennis shoes, I might add, are carefully stored away and never left within olfactory range, for such a *faux pas* might reflect upon their high social standing.

As befits the members of a mighty conglomerate, a vertical integration, if you will, the experts and their assistants at Sotheby Parke Bernet now wear long white coats. They look like lab technicians, but such clinical fripperies inspire confidence!

One of the most amusing parts of the British drama is the huckster's initial appearance on the podium. There is an expectant hush in the audience, a lull in the whispering as the genteel crier walks to the podium. He is immaculately attired and looks precisely like a Harrod's clerk. His spotters are wearing neat jackets and the drama is about ready to unfold.

Why all this mad folderol to peddle their goods? If I gave you ten years to guess how Peter Wilson, one of the bigwigs at Sotheby Parke Bernet, explained the nonsensical trappings, you'd have to throw in the gavel. He said: "Auctions are theater and if you destroy the theater, you destroy the auction." May I be torn to bits by hammerhead sharks if those were not Mr. Wilson's very words.

If you are as ignorant as I, you probably thought you attended auctions to buy art and artifacts and books and manuscripts and other objects so you could own and treasure them and be secure in your investment. And maybe you relish the mad excitement of bidding, the savagery of competition, and the occasional thrill of a nasty dispute on the floor. But theater! Why, theater means costumes and footlights and costly trappings and sets. I am sure you never guessed, until Peter Wilson, Esq. told you, that when you bid at Sotheby Parke Bernet or Christie's you are a participant in a great and solemn farce. Can you imagine how the huckster-in-chief laughs up his sleeve when at a big art sale he looks out at the sea of expectant faces protruding from monkey suits and evening gowns! He'll play the role for you, and if you are lucky you'll understand his chant. If not, be patient, for one of these days I am going to put out a glossary of accents in British for the guidance of those who understand only English. At Sotheby Parke Bernet, I am happy to report, there are some auctioneers who cry the sales in our native tongue. It is a joy to hear them, for they are experts at their job.

For the benefit of the not-too-bright bidders from Japan and Germany and other foreign nations, the Sotheby Parke Bernet gallery has installed a device that decodes the bids from dollars into francs, marks, pounds, lira, and yen. The device is suspended over the auctioneer's head and while in operation makes a soft, whispering sound like the shuffling of many packs of invisible playing cards. The numerals shimmer on and off in bright white lights.

One foreign bidder complained to me, perhaps jocularly: "It takes away all the suspense. Now I know to the penny what I've paid instead of waiting until I get back to my hotel to figure it all out."

This machine is not all to the bad. It has a soothing, hypnotic effect. If the auction proceedings start to crawl and you get bored, all you need do is watch the lights trickle on and off, hark to the seductive rustling, and you will soon slip off into a pleasant trance.

The catalogs issued by the swells are as pretentious as they are sumptuous, often an effort to substitute beautiful printing and illustrations for knowledge. Frequently the descriptions of lots are pieced together with foreign phrases, a patchwork of gobbledygook and accurate information. Just glance through any of the slick Sotheby Parke Bernet or Christie's catalogs on furniture, for instance. Do you dig en chiffonnière, repoussé, tôle peinte, encoignure, chauffeuse, guéridon, écran à pupitre, verre églomise pier? If you can pick your way through this plethora of *aigus* and *graves* you are obviously an expert, probably a furniture dealer.

"The catalogs of Christie's and Sotheby Parke Bernet are not really designed to sell goods," Herb Melnick, a noted numismatist and auctioneer told me. "Their purpose is to get consignments. The goods could be peddled just as effectively with less costly trappings, but the big, splashy catalogs lure the consignors. Many people who own valuable material are more interested in having their collection enshrined in a beautiful catalog than in getting a lot of money for it."

The impressive catalogs of the great auction galleries are like fishing lures. There are lots of glittering, gadgety lures that no self-respecting trout or bass would ever hit, but they are not designed to hook fish. They are designed to hook the fisherman.

But for all the atrabilious words I've written and will write about the British galleries in America, I must confess that I am one of the fishermen who is hypnotized by the sparkle of

their catalogs. And I am entrapped and enchanted by the
magnificence of their gallery exhibits. My wife and I have
charge accounts at Sotheby's and at Christie's and I am often
beguiled into their salesrooms, for they offer the most alluring
of goods. I am truly seduced by this brace of British vamps
and their audacious little sister, the galleries of Phillips, Son
and Neale in New York.

When I decide to sell things from my own collection, I
often succumb to their wiles. Why? Because with all the
many faults of these mighty galleries they are among the finest
in the world. At their elegant podiums one can most
advantageously buy and sell beautiful paintings by the old
masters, china and silver with a soul-rich patina, furniture
that would delight a maharajah, and glorious jewels that
would corrupt an empress. All that's best of beautiful and
bright may be viewed in their halls and battled for in their
salesrooms.

If I have china to sell, or paintings, I turn to Christie's. If
it's jewelry or a rare print or poster, I pin my hopes on
Sotheby Parke Bernet. But then, after all, I am not entirely at
their mercy. I do possess a little bit of knowledge that, though
it may be a dangerous thing, is enough to enable me to
protect myself in my dealings with these great galleries. The
rug in my living room is a Kirman, glowing with colors,
bought by my wife and me at Sotheby Parke Bernet's on
Madison Avenue. The rug in the living room of our country
home is also a Kirman, purchased at Christie's. Both were
bargains. Both are beautiful and are a part of the joy and
happiness of our lives.

When recently I had two choice paintings to sell I put
them up at Christie's and the old galleries did nobly for me.
True; I knew what the paintings were and what their value
was and how to describe them. But Christie's knocked them
down for me. I ignored their effete manners and overlooked

the posturing young ladies behind the counter, for at no place in the world could I have done so well.

And now, having purified my soul by these admissions, I shall continue my frontal assault, my bayonet charge, if you will, on the unpleasant practices and questionable conduct of the British galleries. I shall point out the many things they do that are inimical to their own greatness. And I shall hope they will soon jettison their more unpleasant procedures and vindicate to Americans their birthright as the world's supreme purveyors of beauty.

On Friday, October 21, 1977, Christie's debuted in New York with a resplendent rare book and autograph catalog replete with lush descriptions and photographs. The cagey old London firm was out to make a big splash in the American pond. Their prize lot was a letter of Martin Luther, described as an "Autograph letter signed, in German." But by one of those cruel twists that only a devout ignorance can achieve, Christie's devoted a full-page illustration to the German translation of Luther's letter, penned in a fine clerical hand. The cataloger was evidently not familiar with autographs and had never seen Luther's script. He assumed that the original letter of the great reformer was nothing more than a copy scrawled in Latin. It was with this boner (explained by Christie's as "a printer's error") and a great deal of pomp that Christie's began its struggle to take over the American auction scene.

The auction house that so proudly traces its lineage back to that first, auspicious sale on December 6, 1766, when James Christie knocked down in Pall Mall two chamber pots and a pair of soiled sheets is now out to educate the New York yokels in the refined art of snobbery. I am now profiting from Mr. Christie's example, for in my auction of May 28, 1981, I offered up, with equal pomp, Mrs. Lincoln's private commode.

The cataloging at Sotheby Parke Bernet, at least in the philographic field, is not an improvement over Christie's. To celebrate the bicentennial in 1976, Sotheby Parke Bernet made one of the prize flubs of the last century. Lewis Grassberger of *The New York Post* (February 24, 1976) described the event:

WASHINGTON RELIC: $40,000 or $200?

Two hundred years later, George Washington is still giving the British a hard time.

Sotheby Parke Bernet, the rich man's flea market, has its auctioneer poised today to start the bidding on a scrap of Washington memorabilia which it claims is worth $40,000 to $60,000.

It's purported to be Washington's own copy of his commission as commander-in-chief of the Continental army, written by the secretary of the Continental Congress, Charles Thomson.

Hold the gavel, says Charles Hamilton. Hamilton, a leading signature and handwriting expert here, insists the paper was not written by Thomson and probably not even contemporary with Washington. He says it's worth about $200.

The prestigious and respected Madison Avenue auction house, which was bought in 1964 by Sotheby's of London, says Hamilton's public protesting has done damage to the property and thrown into question whether it can be sold.

There were rumors that the document might be withdrawn from auction. But a statement issued by Parke-Bernet maintained confidence in the paper's authenticity and guaranteed that authenticity to the purchaser.

It said the stand "is based on our own research,

supported by the positive statements made by
disinterested authorities in the field." The gallery
reaffirmed its position last night.

Hamilton, who runs his own auction gallery here, said
that he handled hundreds of Thomson signatures during
his long career (He's 62) and flatly said, "It is definitely
not in Charles Thomson's handwriting.

"His hand was sharp and angular and he rarely, if ever,
crossed a T," said Hamilton. "His handwriting was also
difficult to read. The handwriting in this document is a
fine, cursive, curved clerical hand, very easy to read . . .
entirely different from Thomson's hand . . ."

Parke Bernet's book and manuscript department
described it as "the most significant Washington relic to
come to light in over 100 years."

Dated June 19, 1775, and addressed to George
Washington Esquire, the sheepskin document says, "We
. . . appoint you to be General and Commander-in-Chief
of the army of the united colonies and of all the forces
raised or to be raised for the defense of American
Liberty." The names signed below are Thomson's and
John Hancock, president of the Congress . . .

The Washington commission was the showpiece of a
collection of literary Americana which Parke-Bernet has
been calling the finest sale of its kind. The merchandise
is valued at over a million dollars and also includes a
collection of signed autograph letters written by
Washington, while he was President, to his overseer at
Mt. Vernon.

Sotheby Parke Bernet withdrew the document "in order to
institute further definitive research." What these ses-
quipedalian words mean is that Sotheby Parke Bernet finally

recognized the document as an adventure in fantasy and took it off the market.

Had Sotheby Parke Bernet sold this bogus commission it might have established a new world's record for an autograph document. I met one out-of-town dealer who had come to New York girded with a mighty wallet and prepared to take back the commission with him, no matter what the price.

Phillips, Son and Neale, the New York–British gallery, has not improved upon the inept cataloging of its fellow Britons. I've watched for several years with a sort of grim amusement and without comment its selling of bogus or misdescribed letters and documents. Late in March, 1981, I visited Phillips with my friend, James Camner, to glance over the presale exhibition of some books and autographs in which he was interested. I noticed in Jim's catalog the description of a letter of Sir Walter Scott's, dated 1830, about some illustrations for *Waverly*.

"This is an amusing item," I said to Jim, "because I know it's a fake even before I look at it. I've seen it before."

I asked one of the two pleasant young ladies in the room to bring me the folder containing the letter. She unlocked a glass case and brought it to me.

Jim watched with curiosity as I took the letter out of the folder. "Notice," I said, "that it's a pretty good copy, accurate in most details and with a postmarked address. But," I added, handing the letter to Jim, "just lift it up to the light and read the watermark."

Jim raised the letter and looked at the watermark. It was dated 1832, two years after Scott wrote the letter! "You see," I said, "it was sheer laziness that caused Phillips to catalog this fake as genuine. Presumably they don't know a copy from an original, but certainly the cataloger could have held this letter up to the light and read the watermark."

This type of sloppy, careless, and irresponsible cataloging is typical of the three British galleries.

Both Christie's and Sotheby Parke Bernet are very keen on breaking records, and the seesaw competition between them is a delight to read about. First one grabs the record, then the other. Claims and counterclaims fly as the battle for supremacy in America rages between these two great British firms. Before me lies a *Newsletter* of Sotheby Parke Bernet announcing triumphantly their new records. Among the big-buck victories are a rosewood center table by John Henry Belter ($60,000), highest price ever for a Belter, a painted wooden lion ($40,000), highest ever for a wooden lion, a Latin American painting ($190,000), best price for a Latin American canvas, a Winslow Homer painting ($1,700,000), top figure for a Homer, an Audubon print, "Great Blue Heron" ($30,000), best price yet for an Audubon print, and a watch ($105,000), world-beater for a Swiss ticker. The preoccupation with breaking records is perhaps a symptom of our decadent era. It's how much an object fetches, not how beautiful or important it is, that matters. Nobody today wants to be vulgar and talk about the vibrant, lush, living colors of Van Gogh. Talk like that is passé. Get right to the bottom line: What's his stuff worth in good ol' American bucks?

But America's not the only nation to wince at the Sotheby Parke Bernet–Christie mania for breaking records. In Switzerland, Pierre Koller of the Galerie Koller, long accustomed to the peaceful ways of the traditional European auctions, reacted in December, 1980, to the invasion of Zurich by the two great British auction houses:

Auctioneering has entered a world of different dimensions—one marked by the endless chase after superlatives. Tranquil Europe, where the trading in and

auctioning of art objects had until recently proceeded at a
measured pace, unexpectedly turned into the playground
of hucksters who offered their merchandise, namely art,
to the (initially) startled collector with ever louder
fanfare. At the same time, they proclaim their own
record price sagas at the top of their voices.

The European art market increasingly assumed the
characteristics of the U.S. computer hardselling.
Suddenly, every auction was more successful than the
previous one. At each auction, record prices were
reached in some art category or other. Each sale was
instantly termed "the sale of the years," "the sensation of
the picture market," or "the greatest event of the
season."

Despite their frenetic and rather adolescent competition to
set new records, both Sotheby Parke Bernet and Christie's, I
willingly concede, have done much for the purveyance of art
and antiquities. But they have also introduced into this
country a distasteful note of vulgarity: hearse chasing. Both
galleries have experts who are up on necrology. They read the
obits before they read the news. The death of a general, a
statesman, a great lady, a prominent author, a dissipated old
playboy alerts them into action. An immediate phone call, if
the estate is large and valuable. A letter of condolence,
baited with outstretched palm, if the worth of the deceased is
deemed modest.

Sometimes these two great galleries do not wait for the
death rattle. They visit dying collectors and assuage terminal
pains by the assurance that they will disperse the ailing one's
assemblage of treasures at special discount rates available only
to the mortuary bound.

At Phillips, Son and Neal, an American girl was assigned
the task of reading the obituaries early every morning, then

telephoning the family of the deceased to solicit consignments. It was important to reach the bereaved before
their rivals, Sotheby Parke Bernet and Christie's. "I felt like a
ghoul," the girl said later. "Sometimes the widow would be
sobbing while I explained our special commission arrangement for handling estates. Finally, after three months of this
predatory work I realized I'd never get calloused and asked for
a transfer."

A friend of mine recently told me: "You're a damn fool,
Hamilton, for not sending out consignment letters to the
estates of all the important people who die. You're 67 and so
of course you read the obits every morning to see who you've
outlasted. Why not cash in on your morbid streak? Send a
form letter out to every widow or heir or executor. You can't
lose. All the other big auction houses do it."

"And what form shall my letter to the bereft take?" I
asked.

My friend wrote a sample letter. It was too saccharine, I
thought. I'd read the ghoul-letter used by Sotheby Parke
Bernet and noticed that they wasted no time firing arrows of
condolence at the heart but aimed right for the money belt.
So I wrote an obituary letter. It sounded tasteless, almost
brutal. I set it aside for a week and then re-read it. The
second time around it sounded even worse and I tore it up in
disgust.

That ended my efforts with the "hearse post." I'm just not
emotionally geared to hit on a family in grief.

CHAPTER 3

Dirty Tricks from the Podium

WHAT DO YOU THINK this is worth, Charlie?" Mary
A. Benjamin, the doyenne of the world's philogra-
phers, pointed to a description in the catalog of Part
II of the Philip D. Sang collection.

I studied the photograph of the document in the Sotheby
Parke Bernet catalog, a receipt for a "ride" from Boston to
New York signed by Paul Revere, with a further notation
bearing John Hancock's signature. The catalog noted that the
ride was one on which Revere had carried the news of the
Boston Tea Party.

"Don't tell me, Charlie!" said Mary, as I was about to
venture an opinion. "Write the amount on this slip of paper.
I'll write my estimate on another slip. Then we'll swap slips."

I wrote "$5,000" and we exchanged notes. Mary, I saw,
had written the same figure—$5,000.

Mary said: "They haven't printed an estimate of value in
the catalog, but I'm told they're thinking in terms of $75,000
or thereabouts."

"You're kidding," I said. "Why, this is nothing but a
receipt, not even an account of the ride by Revere. And it's
not a famous ride. Nobody ever heard of it."

Somebody in my gallery had tuned into our conversation
and said: "The word I get is that the estimate on the Revere-
Hancock document was originally about $5,000 and Tom
Clarke, head of the rare book and autograph department,
said: 'I think we can get a lot more for it. Let's try for the big

money.' At Tom's insistence the original estimate was dropped and those three little words, 'Refer to Dept.' that translate into 'lots of dough,' were substituted."

Mary said: "How could Sotheby Parke Bernet make such a mistake?"

"I don't think it was a mistake," I said. "I believe this document is pinpointed for *one* bidder, a specialist in Revolutionary War autographs. You and I hold the opinion that on the open market it's worth $5,000 and certainly wouldn't fetch more than $7,500, but SPB may have a mark in mind and this estimate is geared for him. If he bids, this document may establish a world's record, because my hunch is that SPB has got a whopping reserve (a minimum sale price) on it and anybody who bids is going to be competing against the hidden reserve.

"You know, Mary," I added. "The French have got a new proverb: 'You can sell anything to Americans if you make the price high enough.'"

At the sale that afternoon, on April 20, 1978, the Revere-Hancock document fetched $70,000, a new world's record for an autograph document. That record is still in the *Guinness Book of World's Records*, along with the more recent record established at my gallery (1979) of $100,000 for a Button Gwinnett document.

Not long after the Revere-Hancock receipt smashed the world's records, a similar document, also signed by Revere and Hancock, came out of the woodwork and was offered for sale by the same gallery. This time the man who bought the first document did not take part in the bidding and the second example was bought-in at $7,500 and returned to the owner.

The sales of the larger galleries are often geared for the big bucks crowd. If a certain opulent collector is keen on Lincoln letters, for example, the cataloger for the gallery will point up the features of the Lincoln letters in a sale that will especially

*A new world's record! Document signed by Paul Revere and John Hancock.
Sold at Sotheby Parke Bernet, 1978, $70,000*

wing their way into the mind of the rich mark. Paintings, artifacts, furniture, stamps, and coins are often cataloged with one certain buyer in mind.

"At our sales we know who the crazy bidders are," one noted auctioneer told me. "If we have a bust of Lincoln worth $800, we know there are certain bidders who won't be interested, because it hasn't got a big value, but if we raise the estimate on this same bust to $15,000, these bidders will fight like hell to get it."

One of the special marks of the galleries was the late Sol Feinstone, a delightful and very wealthy old man who had arrived in America as a boy with only 17 cents, or 8 cents, or 14 cents—the amount varied each time he told the story—

and was an avid collector of George Washington letters and memorabilia.

The last time that Sol bought a big lot was when the Long Island Historical Society consigned in 1976 a huge collection of 118 routine letters of Washington on farming matters to Sotheby Parke Bernet. I doubt if Sol would have bought the collection privately. He preferred to bid at auction. Sol was the only possible buyer for this massive collection and he sprang for the reserve of $250,000.

On reflection, however, Sol exhibited the Reynard-the-Fox wits that had brought him his money bags, nearly all by this time given away to worthy causes. In the quiet of his study, fortified with the single glass of wine allowed him by his physician, he contemplated the massive collection of Washington's missives, perused them carefully through his great lenses, and concluded that he'd been overcharged. Nobody had to tell him about the setup. He divined it. Instead of sending the usual prompt check, Sol dallied over the payment with the casual air of a professional deadbeat. Sotheby Parke Bernet waited nervously, keenly aware of Sol's advanced age and hoping that the old philanthropist would not die before he could place his shaky moniker on a check. Sol let them stew. As Sotheby's maintained its anguished vigil at the mail box, the Long Island Historical Society began pleading with Sotheby's for payment to bolster its empty exchequer. Finally the mighty galleries bent a knee to the old man and begged for a remittance.

Sol replied: "I'll give you $200,000 and not a cent more." Sotheby's took it.

Sol was well on in years when he first attended my evening auctions at the Waldorf-Astoria. With his quarter-inch-thick spectacles he looked like a myopic and very wise owl. He carried a magnifying glass with which he studied the catalog during the sale. But he was prone to slumber. By the time our

auctioneer, Gregory Mozian, never remarkable for speed, got
to W for *Washington*, Sol had either tottered out or was
asleep. The result always meant lower prices for our Revolutionary War lots.

"What shall we do?" I asked our vice president, H. Keith
Thompson, Jr.

"Well, we can't stab him with a hat pin or wave smelling
salts under his nose. How about moving *Washington* and the
Revolutionary War up to A for *American Revolution?*"

It was a great inspiration. From that time on Sol was a
voracious bidder and we got higher prices for Washington and
other Revolutionary War lots than any other gallery in New
York.

A neat trick often pulled off by the smaller galleries is
"salting" a celebrated collection with unpedigreed additions.
Suppose the auctioneer is offering for sale the entire furnishings of the sumptuous mansion of the late Lady Alice Fairley.
Her taste, of course, was as impeccable as her ancestry, and
the usual crowd of snobs and socialites will jostle into the
mansion to bid on a few souvenirs from the elegant matron.
The gallery, if dishonest, may salt Lady Alice's mansion with
some paintings, furniture, and books that were acquired from
less distinguished sources, say Jake's Olde Junk Shoppe on
First Avenue. Because of their presumed association with the
grand old dame, these illicit additions will fetch a premium
above their actual value. Famous collections are often
enhanced by salting. When Rudolph Valentino's library was
sold, with other effects of the great actor, right after his
death, it was amazing how many books turned up with
Valentino's book label pasted in them.

The reputable galleries do their salting with no attempt at
dissimulation: "The Lady Alice's superb collection of Tiffany
lamps, with a few additions from other sources."

Occasionally an auction gallery will cooperate with a dealer in establishing spurious values. Suppose an art dealer has picked up at a bargain price 83 suites by Pablo Picasso, the remainder of an edition of 150. The suite (or series) may have a current worth of $1,000 on the art market. However, with the auctioneer as his shill, the dealer may offer one suite at public sale and bid it up to $6,500. He then prices the remaining suites at $3,100 each, noting that "an identical suite fetched $6,500 at auction last month."

This same sort of collusion between auctioneer and dealer (or collector) is often used to establish false values for paintings by a certain artist (of whom the dealer has accumulated a large supply of paintings or on whose work he has a monopoly), limited edition books, stamps, coins, or almost any type of artifact that turns up in quantity.

Some auction galleries are not particular about the brand of warranty that comes with the goods they offer. Bogus authentications often go along with old paintings and furniture.

"It's easy for me to get an authentication for any old painting," a "gentleman dealer" confided recently. "Suppose I've got a painting that's pretty good, a nice little country scene of an inn with a couple of horses and weary travelers done around 1800. Maybe it looks a bit like a George Morland but isn't. I just go to an art expert and tell him: "Look, I think this is a Morland. If it is, I want to pay you $1,000 for authenticating it. If it's not, I think you'll agree that a $100 fee would be more appropriate."

"And the expert exclaims: 'What a beautiful Morland!'

"And so, with this authentication, and maybe one or two more like it, my ersatz Morland goes up on the block, and, despite skepticism from some of the real experts at the sale, is knocked down for a good price."

Exaggerated appraisals of value for use in the auction room may be obtained in the same way. Fortunately most reliable experts do not charge according to the value of the merchandise but have a set fee. I am often offered large sums to commit fraud and I presume other dealers are exposed to the same temptation. My fee does not vary much, however, despite the value of the object I appraise. But any expert who charges on a sliding scale, say one percent or five percent or even an outrageous ten percent of the value of the object appraised, may easily slip into larceny. I once was offered for auction a silver-bound album signed by Queen Victoria, a very attractive little book worth about $500, on which a dishonest appraiser had tacked a value of $50,000. The appraiser's fee was ten percent of his evaluation. He had skinned the owner, an old lady, out of $5,000. When I told her that she had been shamelessly defrauded she began to cry. I gave her a list of agencies to consult regarding her case.

Many lots at auction are accompanied by similar exaggerated appraisals that may beguile collectors into submitting high bids on relatively worthless merchandise.

One of the unpleasant tricks pulled by some galleries is giving exaggerated estimates of value in order to get important consignments. Several years ago I was offered, very tentatively, an early printed copy of the United States Constitution with marginal notations by Pierce Butler, a member of the Constitutional Convention of 1787 from Georgia.

"It should fetch around $150,000 at auction," I wrote the owner. "If you insist upon a reserve, I'll be glad to offer the document on your behalf with a buy-back of $150,000 and, if it doesn't bring that sum, I'll charge you nothing."

Another auction gallery put a higher estimate on the value of the Pierce Butler constitution and got the consignment. After the sale at which the old paper failed to meet its reserve the owner got the constitution back, no doubt with a hefty bill for "cataloging expenses."

"They've got a new little scheme at the big auction houses

now," a friend who often consigns valuable items told me. "The three or four biggest galleries in New York are savage competitors, as you know, and sometimes they exaggerate the value of an article or a collection in order to get me to consign it. I sort of expect that, but I don't like the way they're doing it now. Suppose I take a rare Tiffany watch into Christie's and their expert tells me it's worth $8,000 and should fetch that much at their big jewelry sale coming up soon. Then I take the watch to Sotheby Parke Bernet and they say: 'Oh, we have just the sale to put this into and we can easily get you $10,000 for it,' why, of course, then I'll consign to Sotheby Parke Bernet.

"Now, here's the latest twist. After the gallery, whichever gallery it may be, has got me to sign a contract, they wait a week or two and then call up and say: 'We just spoke with our expert here and he now feels that the value of your Tiffany watch is closer to $6,000. If it's okay with you, we'll just sell the watch with a reserve of $6,000 instead of $10,000.'

"This has happened to me a lot lately and it takes most of the fun out of selling at auction."

Nearly all the lots you buy from the New York galleries will turn out to be pretty much as represented. I've had very little trouble myself, and I've purchased from all the big and little galleries in the city. The warranty of most galleries is a bit on the iffy side, but if you do get stuck with a reproduction or a fake when the gallery claimed it was an original, and the gallery refuses to refund your money, the best recourse is New York's Department of Consumer Affairs on Lafayette Street.

You'll also hear a lot of talk about how the New York galleries don't use mail bids competitively. The claim is sometimes made that if the mail bidder or phone bidder gets anything at all it will be for the top amount of his bid. This may happen occasionally at the smaller houses but almost never at the big galleries.

One of the most annoying dirty tricks of the little auction

houses—and the bigger ones in London—is the "quick knockdown." In this scheme, the auctioneer operates by himself, with a spurious mail bid, or with a confederate in the salesroom, to sell valuable lots cheaply by knocking them down before anyone else has a chance to put in a bid.

"I was at a big auction in January, 1981," a friend complained. "It was one of the oldest galleries in London. And I didn't get a chance to bid on a single thing. The auctioneer was working the quick knockdown."

"Well," I said. "Don't go to those fly-by-night sales."

"This was one of the world's biggest auction galleries! It really sizzled me when the auctioneer blatantly ignored my bids. Finally I raised my hand and yelled at the same time, but the auctioneer turned the other way. When I complained in a loud voice, the auctioneer said tartly: 'Please speak up, sir. We've got to move along. We can't waste all afternoon here.'

"He'd put a lot up and say all in one breath: 'Lot 83, I have 10 guineas. No more?' And his eyes would sweep the room in a one-second glassy, unseeing movement, then: 'Sold, 10 guineas.'

"Of course, I knew he was knocking the stuff down to a partner for a tenth of its value, but neither I nor anyone else in the room could do a damn thing about it."

In his book *Antique Dealer* R. P. Way explains how he and his fellow dealers found a way to stop the quick knockdown by an auctioneer who was also a collector of old china:

His habit, when a sale included a lot he wanted for himself, was to say, for instance, "Lot 16, a pair of Chelsea figures in perfect condition. What am I bid?" And then, before anyone there had a chance to speak, he would begin to gabble at high speed, "10/–, 15/–, 17/–," and then rap down his hammer. If someone shouted a higher bid, this auctioneer would say blandly, "Sorry, too late." He even had the audacity to knock down these pieces to himself under his own name.

However, we found a way of putting an end to his little game. When we knew that a really fine piece of china was coming up for sale, we would arrange for one dealer to shout out, immediately, "Ten pound, Sir," before the auctioneer was able to get in a bid on his own account. Another dealer would follow with a higher bid and this auctioneer, who liked getting his china for next to nothing, would be frightened off.

But don't be misled into thinking that there are many auctioneers of this calibre. All the real auctioneers I knew are men of the greatest integrity.

One of the hardest auction deceptions to uncover is the merchandise switch, widely operated among dishonest galleries that specialize in coins and stamps. If a collection is consigned, let us say, that includes a complete set of Columbian stamps in superb, fresh, uncanceled state, with original gum and wide margins on each stamp, the gallery may substitute a similar set, not so fine, in the sale, taking the superb set for private sale. The difference in value might be as much as $5,000, for in stamps the condition is of great importance. At crooked coin auctions the switching of coins by the gallery is done with ease, and the auctioneer merely substitutes a coin in extremely fine condition for a coin of the same denomination and same date that is in mint condition. The difference in value may be many thousands of dollars, yet to the uninitiate the coins may appear to be almost the same. Even if the consignor, often an executor, keeps a scrupulous inventory of the coins or stamps consigned, he cannot detect that a switch was made, for the difference in condition is too subtle for an amateur to discern. Although coin and stamp auctioneers take only a ten percent commission from the consignor, many of them retire rich at an early age.

Sometimes a crooked auction gallery can turn a quick buck by "misattribution." If they get consigned to them an original etching by Rembrandt, an early issue (or "state") worth perhaps $4,000, they simply "make a mistake" and describe it in their catalog as a modern copy, with a value of about $10. An associate then buys it at the sale or it is "sold to order," and the auctioneer knocks it down to himself. This fraud can be practiced on a more elaborate scale with fine paintings. An original, unsigned watercolor by Thomas Rowlandson, worth maybe $3,500, can be described as an old watercolor, artist unknown, valued at only a few dollars. With extremely valuable paintings, there is always the problem that some expert may spot the misattribution.

The gallery fraud of misattribution is often worked in other fields. A rare first edition is described as a common, later issue of little value; a priceless Chinese vase is offered as a modern reproduction; a beautiful eighteenth-century fauteuil is put on the block as a nineteenth-century copy, and so on. Consignors should make sure that their property is accurately described in the auctioneer's catalog.

Another device of dishonest galleries, in dealing with owners who are not knowledgeable, is to bury a very valuable article—a coin, stamp, vase, book, or other item—in a large lot so that it will be overlooked by bidders who are in quest of only rare or choice items. An extremely rare foreign stamp, for instance, that might be worth $5,000, would be utterly lost in a cheap beginner's lot of 10,000 miscellaneous stamps, valued by the auctioneer at $75. Such a lot would not be examined by an advanced collector and very likely nobody would look it over. The auctioneer or a confederate would buy it for a small sum and then sell the valuable stamp privately. Even if their fraud were uncovered, the auctioneer could explain that the rare stamp was buried by accident in the big lot. The proper description for this sort of dirty trick is *theft*.

Even as this chapter was being copyedited at the publishers (March, 1981) a clever New York auctioneer apparently tried to skin me with the old "burial trick." I'd consigned 161 obsolete stock certificates to his auction of financial memorabilia. In the group were three very rare certificates issued by the first Selznick Movie Studios in 1922. They were signed by the 20-year-old David O. Selznick and worth at least $350. As an expert, the auctioneer should have spotted these rarities and offered them separately. Or at least mentioned them in his catalog description.

Claiming later that he was ignorant of their value, he buried the Selznick certificates with the other 158 papers in an enormous group that he described as a "mixed lot, many common varieties, for the beginning collector," with an estimated value of $150 to $225. Possibly he planned to buy in the lot cheaply for himself.

When I got his catalog and discovered the "burial," I demanded the return of the rare certificates.

"You're an auctioneer," he retorted. "You know I can't break up that big lot now."

I convinced him to take out the three documents. In sending them back, he wrote: "I had asked about one of the Selznicks for my own collection, now that you called my attention to it. If you would care to quote a price . . . I would be happy to hear it."

And with this unpleasant story I come to one of the most unusual auctions of all time—the auction that never was. Back in 1955, my friend, Robert Batchelder, a coin and autograph expert from Ambler, Pennsylvania, got a mail-order auction catalog from a prominent coin dealer, R. H. Burnie of Pascagoula, Mississippi. "It was filled with rare pioneer gold coins," said Bob. "When I looked through that catalog my mouth watered. I never saw so many choice coins in all my life.

"The difficulty was that the collection had been consigned to Burnie by a wealthy eccentric who insisted that a twenty-five percent deposit be sent with all mail bids and that the collection be kept in a safe, unviewed, until the sale was over.

"The conditions of sale were pretty tough, but the coins were so superb that most dealers and collectors went along with the owner's demands.

"I had very little money at the time because I was fresh out of college and just getting started. I couldn't send twenty-five percent for the lots I bid on, but I did manage to scrape together a deposit of $150, which Burnie accepted.

"In fact, he accepted all the deposits sent by dozens of dealers and collectors throughout the country and then skipped off to Mexico, abandoning his wife and child.

"And it turned out that there was no eccentric consignor and there were no rare coins except in Burnie's fertile imagination.

"Burnie was the only guy I ever knew of who got rich out of an auction never held!"

CHAPTER 4

The Peregrinations
of Napoleon's Penis

D O YOU KNOW WHY I've risked my ass so many times
in battle?" said Napoleon to his aide, Bourrienne.
"Not for glory; not for power; not for fame; not for
wealth; not for France. It was for love. As a conqueror I could
possess every beautiful woman I desired."

If you have delved into the tell-all memoirs of the great
general by his valet, Constant, you will be aware that
Napoleon got what he wanted. The escapades of the emperor's penis during his lifetime have beguiled much ink from
the pens of thousands of historians. Few who write about him
can pass up the temptation to recount at least a few dozen or
so of his tempestuous affairs.

Yet the adventures of Napoleon's intimate organ after
death, in and out of the auction room, are fully as exciting as
the romantic encounters so doted upon by novelists and
biographers.

The posthumous career of Napoleon's amorous appendage
began in a dimly lit cottage at Longwood on the island of St.
Helena, a craggy little fist of rock in the South Atlantic.

On the morning of May 5, 1821, the lips of the dying
emperor moved for the last time. General Montholon, his
friend and aide, strove to catch the final sounds and thought
he could make out the word, "Josephine." Then the pale
hands of the famous general trembled ever so slightly and he

51

passed into a deep coma. At 5:49, precisely eight minutes after the sun had disappeared into the sea and just as the crepuscule shimmered over the landscape, Napoleon died. His face in death was beautiful, like a heroic bust of Parian marble.

The men who loved Napoleon and the men who had held him captive knew that the greatest soldier since Hannibal was lying in the little house at Longwood and they got ready for the autopsy that had been requested by the emperor himself. On May 6, in the presence of more than a dozen spectators, including two aides who were devoted to the dead man, Bertrand and Montholon, the Abbé Vignali, a semiliterate priest, and Ali (Louis Etienne Saint-Denis), Napoleon's second valet, the body was opened by the emperor's surgeon, Professor Francesco Antommarchi. He examined the stomach and liver and diagnosed the cause of death as cancer of the stomach. Antommarchi took out the heart and stomach and sewed the body back up.

Ninety-two years later in his Hunterian Lecture, delivered on January 6, 1913, Professor Keith, the conservator of the Museum of the Royal College of Surgeons, commented on specimens in the museum that were supposed to have been removed from the body of Napoleon by Antommarchi. Keith's opinion was that, since the post-mortem lasted for less than two hours, in the continued presence of six doctors and a number of other persons, neither Antommarchi nor anyone else could have cut anything from the body, unperceived, during the autopsy. The eyes of everybody, including Napoleon's faithful aides, were upon the dissector the whole time. Then, as a very detailed official report made on May 6, 1821, by eyewitness Sir Thomas Reade states, the body was closed up in the presence of a dozen witnesses and from that time remained under constant guard and was never again touched.

"It's quite possible," a prominent doctor told me, "that Antommarchi's scalpel could have slipped and cut off Napoleon's penis during the autopsy without attracting undue attention."

But Dr. Michael Baden, New York Medical Examiner, commented: "Such an obvious organ of the body could only be severed deliberately and its amputation would be observed by everyone present."

There is an almost positive method by which this personal appendage could be identified. Many years ago I owned a fully authenticated lock of hair cut from the emperor's head during the St. Helena exile. I presented some strands to Gregory Troubetskoy, a friend and fellow admirer of Napoleon. Gregory had the hair chemically analyzed for arsenic, as there were rumors that Napoleon had been poisoned by his British captors. The analysis revealed a high concentration of arsenic, an amount more than sufficient to cause death. Unlike other lethal poisons, most of which dissipate after death, arsenic remains permanently as a mute witness to murder or suicide.

I've urged the present owner of the penis to have a tissue sample subjected to a neutron activation analysis for arsenic. If there is an abnormal amount of this deadly poison in the tissue, then I see no reason for doubt that the penis is that of the great conqueror.

The Abbé Vignali, a priest so ignorant he believed Alexander the Great to be a Roman general, administered the last rites to Napoleon and conducted his funeral. For these services he was rewarded with a number of objects as souvenirs—some of the emperor's knives and forks, a silver cup, a shirt and handkerchief marked with Napoleon's emblem, a pair of white breeches, a death mask by Antommarchi, and, the pièce de résistance, the penis that had served the emperor so well during his many conquests.

Vignali took his collection of relics back to his home in Corsica, the little island where Napoleon was born. In 1828 he was slain in a vendetta. His sister, Roxane Vignali Gianettini, inherited the relics and at her death passed them on to her son, Charles-Marie Gianettini. In 1916 Vignali's descendants sold the collection to Maggs and Co., a British rare book firm. The nation of shopkeepers of which Napoleon spoke so scornfully had at last got an article of commerce worth boasting about! They had achieved a neat and vulgar vengeance upon the great warrior who had harrassed and humiliated them for more than two decades.

In 1924, Dr. A. S. W. Rosenbach, the high cockalorum of American bibliophiles, journeyed to England on a buying trip and for only £400 ($2,000) acquired from Maggs all the Vignali relics including "the mummified tendon taken from Napoleon's body during the post-mortem."

Although I've been told that Dillinger's penis is preserved in a glass bottle at a Midwestern university, that bizarre relic has never titillated the world like the romantic tool that Dr. Rosenbach proudly carried home from London. The tendon's claim to authenticity rested mainly on a memoir by the valet, Ali (Saint-Denis), published in 1852 in the celebrated *Revue des Mondes*. Ali claimed that he and Vignali had removed certain unnamed portions of Napoleon's corpse during the autopsy.

Back in Philadelphia, Dr. R. delighted the press with his acquisition, now enshrined in an elaborate case of blue morocco and velvet, and featured it in a new catalog to the delectation of his more prurient clients.

Three years later the doctor displayed the penis, with other Vignali relics, in the Museum of French Art. A New York newspaper commented: "Maudlin sentimentalizers sniffled; shallow women giggled, pointed. In a glass case they saw something looking like a maltreated strip of buckskin shoe-

lace or shriveled eel." Cruel words about the private weapon
with which Napoleon had hoped to found a French dynasty!

After two decades of ownership Dr. Rosenbach sold the
tendon to Donald Hyde, a collector remembered for his great
assemblage of books and letters of Dr. Samuel Johnson.

When Hyde died his wife, Mary, turned the collection
over to Dr. Rosenbach's capable successor, John Fleming.

At this juncture a youthful and very exuberant dealer and
close friend of mine, Bruce Gimelson, asked me for an
introduction to Fleming. He got the introduction and, in
very short order, he also got the Vignali collection at a price
(about $35,000) that forever rendered it unsalable at a profit.

"Would you like to sell the collection for me at one of your
auctions?" Bruce asked me.

"Let me think about it," I said. That evening I discussed
the relics with Diane. She felt that it would be in very poor
taste to offer the penis at auction. "You're already branded as
a maverick because you've sold letters of Lee Harvey Oswald.
You've got to stop somewhere and I think this is where you
should draw the line."

The next day I told Bruce: "I'll auction everything except
the short arm."

"No dice. The collection stays together. The penis is the
most spectacular relic and it gives greater value to the rest of
the items."

A year or so later, after a few sporadic and unsuccessful
efforts to vend the collection and after taking on a partner to
help absorb the cost, Gimelson put the whole works up for
sale at Christie's in London, a gallery that haughtily eschews
the sale of Nazi relics but did not shrink from peddling a great
man's penis.

In the itemized collection of Vignali, offered as one huge
lot, appears the entry: "A small dried-up object, genteelly
described as a mummified tendon, taken from his [Na-

poleon's] body during the post-mortem. The authenticity of
the macabre relic has been confirmed by the publication in
the *Revue des Mondes* of a posthumous memoir by St. Denis,
in which he expressly states that he and Vignali took away
small pieces of Napoleon's corpse during the autopsy."

The recommendation to auction the collection at Christie's was made to Gimelson by an American expert who,
according to the Chicago dealer, Ralph Newman, "has made
a career out of being inept." In this case the "expert" proved
very inept, for Christie's reneged on its offer to set a reserve
on the collection and Gimelson was forced to "buy it in" at
£19,000 (about $35,000). Christie's charged him five percent
of the buy-in price for its abortive effort.

Bruce and his new bride, Josephine Dunninger, a delightful
young lady, had attended the sale in London. When the
penis failed to sell, a British tabloid carried the lurid headline:
NOT TONIGHT, JOSEPHINE!

And so the penis, now looking like a shriveled seahorse,
returned across the ocean to Philadelphia.

For nearly eight years it languished in the archives of Bruce
Gimelson who had, meanwhile, moved to more sumptuous
quarters, worthy of the relics, in Chalfont, Pennsylvania.
Bruce decided to sell the collection in Paris and to offer the
items individually, a decision he should have made years
earlier. He consigned all the Vignali material to the famed
gallery *Drouot Rive Gauche*. But when it came to describing
Napoleon's penis in the catalog, the nation of great lovers,
long accustomed to explicit language, cowered before the
shadow of the little corporal. They fell back on the feeble
euphemism "tendon" and devoted only a few ambiguous
words to Lot 54, the stellar item in the sale.

This time the penis found a new owner, one more qualified
to give it a much needed clinical scrutiny. Bidding through

Gimelson, the world's leading urologist bought the romantic relic for about $3,000 in French francs.

Less than a year after the sale in Paris, on July 31, 1978, *People* magazine published a profile of me and misquoted a few facetious comments I'd made on the penis: "With fierce pride, Hamilton began to set standards. He was the first and he is still the only dealer in documents to guarantee 'forever' the authenticity and clear title of every piece he auctions. Offered an item widely believed to be Napoleon's penis—the doctor who did the autopsy is said to have kept it as a souvenir—Hamilton refused to auction it. 'The years had not been kind to the object,' he explains, 'and it was impossible to authenticate it as a part of Bonaparte. I understand the French government later acquired the thing and buried it with Napoleon in Les Invalides.'"

The first part of this statement I did not make. But the second part, about the penis's interment with the balance of Napoleon's corpse, was uttered in jest, with a wry smile. If the writer of the profile, who spent several full days interviewing me, had looked into my eyes at the time he would have noted a mischievous twinkle. The truth is, I had no information on the purchaser or the final destination of the fabled penis.

My friend, Bruce Gimelson, was roused by the article into writing a fierce denunciation of my scholarship to *People* magazine. After some preliminary comments on my exhorbitant commission rates, small income (Lord, how true!), and brushes with Jacqueline Onassis, Bruce came to the point:

> I owned Napoleon's penis along with the rest of the famous Abbe Vignali Collection of Napoleonic relics. While Mr. Hamilton is a recognized expert in the autographs of historic personages he is by no means

conversant with their private parts. This particular appendage was mentioned in various scholarly journals throughout history including an 1852 edition of *Revu Du Monde, Rosenbach* by Wolf and Fleming, etc. Of course, as Hamilton says, "the years had not been kind to [it] . . ." but if in 200 years an historian has the opportunity to examine Mr. Hamilton's private remains, I am sure the same statement could be made (in a much shorter context, of course). The personal appendage of the emperor was subsequently sold in a Paris auction, thoroughly authenticated by Robert-Jean Charles, not to the French government, but to a New York collector who is, in fact, one of Mr. Hamilton's better customers.

A young lady from *People* called me on the phone and read the letter of Gimelson to me. "Naturally," she said, "we won't publish this letter without your permission."

I gave my permission.

"Can you make a very brief rebuttal for publication on Mr. Gimelson's claim that the penis of Napoleon is unquestionably authentic?"

"Sure," I said. "Only Josephine would know for certain."

CHAPTER 5

How Bidders Cheat the Galleries

I WOULDN'T BID ON that if I were you!" An old dealer sidled up to me and put a stubby finger on the document I was examining at one of the big galleries. "I think that's a secretarial signature." He pointed to the mark of King Philip, the Indian chief. "Philip never learned to handle a quill," he went on. "Besides, this old deed looks awfully official, probably stolen out of some archive or library."

"I see nothing wrong with the signature," I said, looking carefully at the tilted P-mark of the noted warrior. "But I'll bear your advice in mind."

The dealer ambled off and a few minutes later I saw him whispering the same warning to a collector who had also picked up the King Philip document.

For economic reasons, I decided not to bid on the King Philip, a great rarity worth over a thousand dollars. But I was not astonished when most of the audience "sat on their hands." The crafty old dealer who had spread the warning snared the rare Indian signature for a tithe of its worth. He'd pulled off one of the oldest and sneakiest tricks in the trade. By denigrating the Philip document and casting doubt on its authenticity and provenance he'd short-circuited the bidding and picked up a great bargain.

This is a favorite ploy in the world of art and artifacts, and many a great painting by an old master has been knocked down for a pittance after a slander campaign by one or more dealers looking for a "steal."

Another way to defraud the auction house and its consignors, one frequently used by petty thieves, is their trick of shifting rare items from one auction lot to another, when not observed, during the pre-sale exhibition, preferably just before the auction so that the fraud will pass unnoticed. A scarce letter or print, a piece of china, a watercolor, a coin, or a stamp can be deftly transferred without detection from Lot 39, let us say, to Lot 40, both of which may consist of half a dozen or more items. If the trick is uncovered, then it passes off as nothing more than a little mix-up in replacing the items after examination.

When the sale is over the cheat pays for and picks up Lot 40, which he has bought at a low price, and in which he has previously planted the one valuable item from Lot 39, having replaced it with a virtually worthless item from Lot 40. Thus both lots have the requisite number of items, as indicated in the catalog, but the really valuable item was moved to accommodate the thief. This shabby trick is generally the recourse of cowards who do not have the courage to commit open theft.

Still another menial trick of the light-fingered is to purloin, during the pre-sale exhibit, a small object from a lot consisting of a group of related items, such as one book from a thirty-five–volume set, one card from a rare deck, the lid from a valuable china teapot, a single print from a scarce suite, and then, at the sale, point out that the lot is incomplete and buy it for a fraction of its value.

Other petty thieves, present at nearly every exhibition, slyly pilfer clock keys, or keys to desks or boxes or chests, rare carved knobs or brasses from drawers, and then, after the auction, approach the buyer of the lots, saying: "I think I have a key that will fit that little chest you just bought" or "I've got a knob exactly like the one that's missing from the bureau that was knocked down to you." They make a modest "income" by selling stolen merchandise to the purchasers of articles rendered incomplete by their thefts.

In his book, *Antique Dealer* (London, 1956), R. P. Way admits to participating in a bidder fraud with a fellow dealer named Wakefield. At an auction sale Wakefield discovered "a cabaret set, consisting of a small teapot, milk jug, sugar bowl, and two cups and saucers, all on an oval porcelain tray decorated with roses. This little service was cataloged as French, but Wakefield, having arrived early in the morning, had found that the oval tray was marked with the impressed Swansea mark, so he had stuck a piece of paper over the mark and written over it £3 10s, as though this were a recent selling price for the service.

"At that time a French cabaret service would be worth about £10, but if marked Swansea not less than £60. Naturally as he and I were the only dealers who knew about the paper we had a very good buy."

It is rare that a dealer or auctioneer will admit to fraud, and I must confess that I respect Way for his candid revelation. He died blind and, because of this misfortune and because he so openly wrote of his trickery, I shall allow him to present his *apologia* here: "I suppose to the layman there comes the thought that a lot of sharp practice goes on amongst antique dealers and they perhaps wonder why there is no honour amongst thieves, so to speak. Well, looking at the question from an outside point of view I can see it must appear like that sometimes. But the ethics of it are, I think, based on the following economics. It's a hard life in which to make a good living and the idea of every man for himself has come to be considered perfectly natural. It's a game we play, a gamble— and, as in love and war, it seems to us fair. Every antique dealer has the same chance and if he pits his wits against an opponent and wins, well, that's the luck of the game. If his opponent wins by pulling a fast one, well, one hopes to get even with him the next time."

Anyone who's ever attended a sale in New York, especially at one of the medium-sized galleries, must be aware that there's a lot of chicanery on the part of bidders. They destroy or hide tag numbers so as to discourage or mislead their rivals. They shift numbers on lots to create confusion among their opponents. If there is an especially rare or choice item, they may hide it carefully in a mass of unimportant things, or behind a big table or desk, so that other collectors won't discover it and bid on it. At my autograph sales, the sneaky bidder, not really guilty of any criminal act, simply refiles a folder of autographs in the incorrect spot, making it difficult for other potential bidders to find and examine it.

The classic method of defrauding an auction gallery and its consignors, now a criminal offense in England and very possibly actionable under the fraud laws in the United States, is the "knock-out" or "ring," designed to swindle the gallery by controlling the bids. Here is the description of how an English ring operates, published by Thomas Rohan in his *Confessions of a Dealer* (London, 1924):

> Suppose ten dealers have formed themselves into a Ring, that is to say, into a conspiracy to cheat owners of property out of the true value of their possessions; and suppose that these ten conspirators attend a sale and there find a picture which is worth a fortune. The usual procedure is as follows: A meeting is held before the sale, and the matter is debated. How much is the picture likely to fetch in this auction? Let us say that it is agreed the price will be around £100. It is then settled that one of the dealers who wants the picture shall bid for it, and he is styled the King of the Knock-Out.

The picture is put up, Lot 21, let us say, and the nervous bidders glance at the formidable dealers from London to try to discover what they think about it. Those professional faces express indifference, contempt, or active dislike. At last someone bids £50. The King of the Knock-Out, as if he is willing to risk a few pounds on a doubtful picture, makes an advance of £5. The bids proceed, the rest of the dealers laughing or jeering among themselves, and at last the valuable picture is knocked down to the King for, let us say, £100.

After this "steal," the knock-out chief supervises the private auction of the painting to the members of the ring. If it sells for, say, £1,000, then the new purchaser puts the £1,000 into a kitty, from which the original buyer at the first sale takes the amount he paid for the painting, £100, and the balance of £900 is divvied up among the ten cheats, each of whom gets £90.

Despite the prevalence of the ring in the towns and shires of merry England, the news of its operation apparently came as a surprise to *The London Sunday Times*, for on November 8, 1964, they published an article about "The Curious Case of the Chippendale Commode" in which was chronicled the operations of a ring in a town about a hundred miles northwest of London. Bidding was slow and desultory and the Chippendale commode was finally knocked down for £750. The disinterest of the dealers and the sporadic bidding should have tipped off onlookers that the ring was at work. Later it turned out that the trustees of the estate and the auctioneer were totally gulled by the ring. The auctioneer must have been a hayseed not to know what was going on.

In the evening of the sale day, the commode was re-auctioned in a private knock-out sale open only to the several dozen members of the ring. The lots bought at the original sale by the chief of the knock-out were sold at prices far in advance of what they fetched earlier in the day. The commode brought £4,350. The immense profit was split equally among the ring members.

After the split, however, some of the dealers remained to participate in a second private sale. This new sale was possible because, when there are a number of small dealers involved in the ring operation, it's customary for the king of the knock-out to ask these persons to "defend themselves" by actively bidding at the ring sale on some of the minor items. If the small dealers are short of cash they fail to meet the test and are paid off immediately. As the items become more expensive—the costly articles are saved for the last—others are forced to drop out. Only a few dealers are left for the final sale of the major items or item.

By the time the commode was sold for £4,350 to one of the dealers in the ring, some of the minor participants had been paid off and had gone home. Only five of the richest and most voracious of the dealers stayed to compete for the grand prize, the rare Chippendale commode. After ferocious bidding, the commode was finally knocked down for £10,000. The additional profit, slightly more than £1,000 each, was split equally among the five thieves.

In the shires of England there are still many small dealers who rarely buy or sell any antiquities but who make a modest living by following the country auctions and taking part as members of the ring.

Although the ring is an established institution in Great Britain, operating with great success at smaller sales and with ever increasing difficulty at the big auctions, it has never worked very effectively in the United States. A few years ago the ring was an effective method of fraud at stamp and coin sales. But today, with the growing number of bidders, the independence of many big buyers, and the animosity that exists among dealers, with many loners who snarl and snap at each other, it is virtually impossible for the ring to get a foothold in America.

There is one trick that does work and often results in lower prices at auction. That's the mythical "Big Bid." All it takes to pull off the Big Bid ploy is chutzpa and an authoritative manner. Let us say that the target is an Einstein manuscript, worth about $15,000. The person pulling off the Big Bid trick spreads a story like this: "The government of Israel has a representative here to bid on the Einstein manuscript. I was talking yesterday with a friend of his and he says that Mr. Lazarus, the man from Israel, is authorized to go to $65,000, if necessary, to get the Einstein. He admits it's only worth $10,000 but it fits right in with the Einstein collection in Israel. 'I'm not going home without it,' is what Mr. Lazarus said yesterday."

A lot of potential bidders, hearing this story, would be discouraged and might drop out as bidders, but if anyone says, "Well, I'm going to bid on it anyway," then the person spreading the Big Bid story comes back with, "You'll make a fool of yourself if you try to compete against Lazarus."

The result: The Einstein sells for its opening bid of $5,000 since all the competition has been bluffed out.

The Big Bid ploy works in many different ways but is especially effective with paintings when the rumor is spread that the Guggenheim, or the Getty Museum, or Norton Simon, or some other fabled collector or institution is going after the whole group of Picassos and "anybody who tries to compete with big shots like that has to be off his rocker."

Even auction goers with long experience have fallen for the Big Bid ploy and refrained from bidding on desirable lots they'd hoped to buy. I've seen persons who were suckered by

"Both parties deprecated war; but one of them would make war rather than let the nation survive; and the other would accept war rather than let it perish. And the war came."

Abraham Lincoln.

Lincoln explains the Civil War in a single sentence! Handwritten, signed excerpt from his Second Inaugural. Sold at Hamilton Galleries, 1979, $13,000

this trick pack up and leave the salesroom before the lot they want even comes up for sale. And so, of course, the inventor of the Big Bid story gets the lot for a fraction of its value.

Perhaps the most common method of swindling the auction gallery is collusion, by which several dealers get together to control prices. "If you lay off the first Lincoln letter, so I can buy it at my price, I'll promise not to run you up on the second one." This sort of arrangement, resulting in lower prices at the sale, is often made by otherwise reputable dealers.

A more flagrant type of collusion is the deliberate attempt to persuade other collectors to refrain from bidding so that a lot will be knocked down for a fraction of its value.

In the fall of 1979 an eighty-seven-year-old man consigned to my gallery for sale a remarkable autograph album in which Lincoln had penned an excerpt of five lines from his famous Second Inaugural Address, one of the world's greatest speeches. I told the old fellow, who was badly in need of money: "This is an historic album, worth at least $10,000. No need to hobble it with a buy-in or reserve."

"You have my complete confidence," he said. "Handle it any way you wish."

As it turned out, my failure to place a reserve or stop-bid on the Lincoln quotation was a serious blunder.

A few days before the sale, I received an $18,000 mail bid on the Lincoln album from an old and reliable client in California. This bid confirmed my private opinion that the Lincoln quotation was not only unique but an extremely important document of museum quality.

The afternoon before the sale, Charles W. Sachs, a Beverly Hills dealer renowned in philographic circles for his acerbic wit, and an old friend of mine, arrived in New York, examined the Lincoln album, and told me privately that he was authorized to execute a coin dealer's bid on it for $20,000.

That evening Sachs and Diane and I had dinner together.

Sachs said: "I hope you don't mind, but I've discovered that you have a bid from California of $18,000 on the Lincoln and I'm going to call the bidder and ask him as a personal favor to me to withdraw his bid so that I won't have to pay a high price. He can't get it anyway, since I've got a bid of $20,000, and there's no point in him forcing my client to pay a lot."

I was sure that Sachs was joking and his remark brought a quick smile from me. Sachs was certainly aware that the cancellation of my mail bid from California might result in a loss of thousands of dollars to my elderly client and me. Thus

I gave as much credence to his remark as if he had said: "Tomorrow I'm going to rob your cash box in the gallery."

The next morning I learned from my secretary that the California bidder had telephoned and withdrawn his $18,000 bid. But this did not alarm me, for I assumed he had turned the bid over to some dealer, perhaps even Sachs, to handle on his behalf in the salesroom.

The arrival of Ralph Newman, the noted Lincoln expert from Chicago, on the afternoon of the sale further reassured me. I was certain that Ralph had made the trip for the express purpose of carrying home in his briefcase the great Lincoln document.

As the sale got underway, my elderly consignor, who was in the audience, fidgeted nervously. "Relax," I said. "Nothing will go amiss." And I put my arm over his shoulder.

Only a few minutes before the Lincoln was to go on the block, Ralph Newman shook hands with me.

"Are you leaving already?" I asked, puzzled that he had passed up the Lincoln album.

"I've got to get back to Chicago," said Ralph. His face was somber and I feared he had received bad news. The bad news, I later learned from Ralph, was the flying rumor of the Big Bid, a rumor that Sachs had circulated that he was prepared to go to $20,000, if necessary, to capture the Lincoln. This was a larger sum than Ralph was prepared to pay.

As usual, I left for my apartment at the intermission and it was not until several hours later that I learned what had taken place at the sale.

Sachs had deftly disposed of all competition except for one dealer who refused to believe in the Big Bid. However, the Lincoln was knocked down to Sachs for only $6,500. Sachs was jubilant. But the old man who owned it began to sob and quietly wipe his eyes with the sleeve of his jacket.

On thinking over the auction results, I made the decision

to void the sale and to ban Sachs from my future auctions.

The next morning, punctuating my remarks with a barrage of four-letter army terms that I hadn't used so vehemently in years, I informed Sachs of my determination. His defense: "I told you two days ago what I intended to do and you didn't object. Moreover, I don't see that I have broken any law."

The coin dealer in California, who claimed he was now the rightful owner of the Lincoln, called and asked me to deliver his property.

I told him: "I'm putting it up for sale again."

He said: "You're making too much of a little thing. Why, this sort of arrangement between dealers goes on at coin sales all the time. It's standard procedure."

"Not at my sales it's not," I said, thinking of the old man who cried.

When the coin dealer's attorney mailed me an ominous and threatening letter, the last of my amiability was crushed out of me and I decided, and my own lawyer concurred, that the case was now one for referral to the United States attorney for criminal action, since the act of collusion had been consummated across state lines.

I quickly made an appointment for a conference with the United States attorney in New York City. He examined with great care every document relative to the case, including a signed affidavit from the California dealer who had withdrawn his bid at Sach's request. Then he picked up the letter from the coin dealer's attorney: "This threatening communication is beneath contempt," he said. "My advice is, don't even answer it.

"I am further convinced," he went on, "that collusion has occurred and that the act of collusion is illegal. But I am not sure precisely which of our federal laws covers this particular case.

"Why don't you, for the moment, let matters go along as

they are. If any further threat is made against you, let me know and we will see precisely what avenues for criminal prosecution are open to the federal government."

But I never heard again from Sachs or his client. On my lawyer's advice I put the Lincoln up for sale again and this time, without the California bidders and with Ralph Newman abstaining, the great document was knocked down for $13,000 to an entirely new bidder.

And the old man hugged me with joy.

CHAPTER 6

The Phantom Bidders

NEXT TIME YOU GO to an auction take a look at the pillars in the salesroom. These pillars are not only graceful architectural devices that support the ceiling. They may also support the auctioneer. When things get tough and no bids come from the floor, or the bids come too slowly, the man with the ivory hammer may call upon the pillars for a bid.

"Do I hear five hundred?" he will cry out, pointing a finger at one of the pillars. Then, turning to a live bidder, if he has one, he will announce: "I have the five hundred. Will you make it five-fifty sir?" And if the live bidder tumbles, the auctioneer may again supplicate his faithful shills, Mr. Ionic and Mrs. Doric.

If there are no pillars in the salesroom, the auctioneer may address the chandelier (always good for a few bids in time of need), an empty seat, a group of standing spectators, or even a tranquil non-bidder.

A friend of mine from the West Coast once journeyed to New York to compete for an item of superlative importance at one of the larger galleries. He brought with him a potent bid from a wealthy client—$100,000. Only after he was seated in the salesroom did he learn the distressing news that a "combine" of speculators in Philadelphia, new at the game, had dispatched a rotund member to the sale armed with a $120,000 bid. So proud was the fat man that he made the mistake of telling anybody who'd listen the amount of his bid.

The news even filtered into the ears of the auctioneer. When the superlative lot was put on the block, the auctioneer announced: "I have a reserve of $100,000 on this lot. Do I hear $100,000? Anyone, $100,000?"

My West Coast friend told me later: "Obviously I had to make the first bid. If the man from the combine got in a bid for $100,000 I was finished. On the other hand, there was a remote chance that he'd wilt at the last moment, so I nodded."

"I have the $100,000," said the auctioneer. "Do I hear one hundred and five?"

The man from the combine thrust a finger into the air.

The auctioneer turned to my friend. "One ten, sir? Will you go one ten?"

My friend shook his head. Looking right at him and ignoring the negative gesture, the auctioneer cried: "I have the one ten." And he turned to the pudgy Philadelphian. "It's one ten against you, sir. Will you make it one twenty?"

The speculator lifted a fat finger and the auctioneer paused for a moment, then slammed his hammer down and said softly: "Sold for $120,000."

After the sale, my friend, aware that the bidder from Philadelphia had been swindled out of $15,000, jested to the auctioneer: "Aren't you going to cut me in for a few thousand for acting as your shill?"

There's a moral here: Never tell anybody the amount you intend to bid on any lot.

However, the crooked auctioneer, operating with one or more live shills, does not need to know your bid limit. If he's an old hand at "running," he can size up a mark and get a pretty good idea of how much he'll spring for. Then he whips his victim into a fever with the excitement of rapid-fire fake bids from every corner of the salesroom. Usually his live shills, if he has any, are partially hidden by curtains or pillars, or in a group of standing spectators. The bidder who seeks to discover who's running him up will often reconnoiter in vain or may see nothing more than the blur of a fast-moving hand signaling a raise.

One afternoon in 1978 I drifted into an antique furniture sale at a great New York gallery just to watch and relish the show. I sat next to a man whose face was vaguely familiar to me and who addressed me by name.

"What do you think this lot will fetch, Mr. Hamilton?" he asked, pointing to the photograph of a regency table in his catalog. The estimate was $3,500 to $4,000. My acquaintance had penciled in his limit: "Go to $4,000."

"You might get it for four," I whispered.

A few minutes later the regency table was paraded out on the stage. The bidding opened at $2,000, very probably the reserve set by the owner, and worked up slowly by $250 increments until it reached $3,000.

I had the uneasy feeling that the auctioneer was drawing raises from a phantom bidder in a small cluster of people at his right near the front of the salesroom. In such a group it was hard to see who, if anyone, was actually bidding. The auctioneer asked the invisible bidder for $3,500 and got it.

Then he pointed to my acquaintance: "$4,000?" My friend nodded.

"Well," I thought, "here's the moment of truth. Since the auctioneer doesn't know about my friend's $4,000 limit, he'll pull a phony bid from the crowd and ask my acquaintance for another raise. What's he going to do when my friend drops the winning bid on his phantom bidder?"

The auctioneer quickly elicited a $500 raise from the little group at his right.

He pointed to the man sitting with me: "$5,000?"

My acquaintance shook his head.

"By George," I thought, "I want to see that clever huckster squirm out of this one."

The auctioneer turned to the phantom bidder and said:

"Sold to—What's that, sir? You didn't give me that last raise? I thought I saw your hand go up."

He turned back to my acquaintance. "Sold to you, sir. $4,000."

I congratulated my new friend and walked out of the great salesroom for a breath of fresh air.

Bruce Gimelson, noted autograph expert from Chalfont, Pennsylvania, was a philographic fledgling in 1967 when he bid at a big New York sale of Western Americana. But if Bruce was not yet in tune with some of the auction practices in New York, he also was not prepared to get swindled.

The auctioneer at the sale was an unctuous newcomer with a British accent, a slick, high-powered huckster out to bleed the Yankees. He spotted Bruce as a greenhorn and decided to run him up.

Bruce entered the fray with a $40 bid on a Confederate book that nobody else seemed to want.

With quick, abrupt gestures and clipped British diction the auctioneer coaxed the bidding up and in only a few moments knocked the lot down to Bruce for $160.

And with the brashness of youth, Gimelson challenged the auctioneer. He shouted: "I'll give you a thousand dollars if you can show me the underbidder!"

"He's that chap back there by the pillar."

The entire audience of three hundred turned and stared at the man in the rear of the room, leaning against a pillar. The man shrugged and said: "It wasn't me. I wasn't bidding."

"The lot's withdrawn, then," said the auctioneer, angrily.

"You can't do that," complained Bruce. "I'm bidding for a customer."

The president of the gallery was in the room. He said to the auctioneer: "Give the lot to the kid for $40."

A few weeks later the gallery fired the new auctioneer.

Sometimes a phantom bidder can get totally out of control and with amusing results. A cagey old warhorse of the galleries told me about an incident he watched at a big salesroom in New York.

"The bidding was hot, really hot," he said. "Here was this spidery guy, an awfully thin, odd-looking character with a zany moustache that drooped unevenly, bidding without a word, not even a grunt, just holding his hand straight up in the air as if he were hailing a taxi. He looked like a real hick, a country goose ready for plucking. I couldn't see the guy bidding against him, but the two of them kept at it until the bid got up to $1,400—and all for an old vase estimated at $75!

"I could tell from the way the spider man never moved that he was determined to get the vase, regardless of what price it fetched. His statue-of-liberty bidding stance also tipped off the auctioneer that he was out to win the lot. Just when everybody in the room was relishing the fray and we were all craning our necks to see who was running the thin man up, the invisible bidder dropped out and the auctioneer cried: 'Going once; going twice; sold, $1,500,' and he pointed to the spider man.

"'Just a minute, Mr. Auctioneer,' said the skinny bidder. 'Put that lot up again, please, and this time no bids from the chandelier.'

"The auctioneer turned red and yelled: 'What do you mean, sir!'

"'Exactly what I said,' came back the thin man.

"We all started to applaud for the spider man. Everybody in the room. We cheered and clapped and stamped our feet because almost everyone suspected what the auctioneer had been up to. Nothing's worse than a crook except an obvious crook.

"So the auctioneer finally put the vase back up again. Nobody was going to bid against the thin man and he bought it for his opening offer of $50."

CHAPTER 7

The Knocking Down of Old Abe

T HE MAD SCRAMBLE for relics of Old Abe got started with a bang. From the moment that Booth's derringer rang out in Ford's Theatre the souvenir hunters went berserk. They shredded the upholstery in Abe's loge. They cut up the flag that hung from his box. They ripped up the carpet and fought over bits of it. They begged for bloody swatches of the taffeta dresses worn by Mary Lincoln and the actress Laura Keene who had cradled the dying president in her lap. They bid eagerly for bits of crimson-stained cloth from a small boy who had sopped up the red drops left by Abe's limp body as it was carried into a tailor's home. They sliced up the blood-soaked towels and bandages used by his doctors. They snipped the hair from his head, still wet with blood, only moments after he died. They even slashed off scraps of the wallpaper in the death room.

It was, and is, a wild orgy of relic hunting. The ghouls of history and the mosquitoes of greatness still swarm when Lincoln mementoes are put on the block. Abe is a perpetual record breaker, a begetter of top prices. Anything he owned, anything he touched, anything he penned is fair game. Even the market for fake relics and forged documents thrives among the true believers who are willing to jettison all skepticism to draw near the great man, to be close to him.

The rabid pursuit of Lincolniana that started on the night of his murder reached its first grand climacteric on February 19, 1952, when the famed collection of Oliver R. Barrett was put up for grabs at Parke-Bernet Galleries in New York. So extensive and exciting were Barrett's "holdings" that Carl Sandburg had written an entire book about them, and their impending dispersal was trumpeted throughout the land.

I was fresh at the auction game and dubious about the effect of such a mass of Lincoln material on the market. To Forest H. Sweet, an oldtime dealer in Battle Creek, Michigan, I offered a prognostication: "The Barrett sale will glut the market with Lincolniana for the next half century and will depress prices down to the level of 1890. There aren't enough Lincoln collectors to absorb such a huge number of letters and documents and relics."

Sweet disagreed. As usual, I was wrong. The Barrett sale annihilated all previous record prices. Madness took over in the salesroom and collectors bid like lunatics escaped from an asylum. Even routine Lincoln commissions that had long been traded among dealers and collectors for a few dollars blossomed into hundred-dollar trophies. Here are a few of the prices, remarkable in their day when a dollar was worth one hundred cents:

A silver watch that Lincoln gave his cousin, Dennis F. Hanks, in 1864, with an affidavit by Hanks, $1,600

A small fragment of Lincoln's tablecloth on which he partook of his wedding breakfast, $30

The great seal of the President of the United States, used by Lincoln on official documents, $650

A quill pen, said to be Lincoln's (Abe preferred a steel-nibbed pen), $65

A gold watch chain presented to Lincoln by a committee of the Union Pacific and Central Pacific railroads, $650

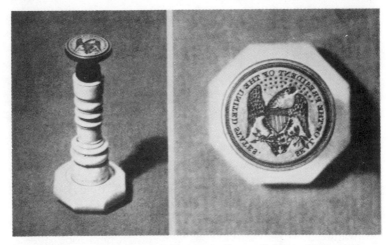

Lincoln's own presidential seal. Sold at Parke Bernet Galleries, 1952, $650, and at Hamilton Galleries, 1967, $12,000

A silk bookmark embroidered with Lincoln's name, $650

A pair of beaded moccasins embroidered with Abe's initials, $275

The Thirteenth Amendment (abolishing slavery), on parchment, signed by Lincoln, Hamlin, and about 150 members of congress, $4,400

Franking signature of Lincoln as postmaster of New Salem, Illinois, $1,600

Page from Lincoln's sum book, $3,600

Lincoln's copy of the Lincoln-Douglas debates, with many corrections in Lincoln's hand, $24,000

A tiny swatch of Laura Keene's dress, worn on the night of Lincoln's murder, $70

The blood-stained fan used by Mrs. Lincoln in Ford's
   Theatre, $70

A ticket to Ford's Theatre for April 14, 1865, the night
   of the murder, $25

The key to the presidential box, $150

A piece of the flag draped over Lincoln's box, $85

A playbill for *Our American Cousin* dated the night of
   Lincoln's assassination, $175

Mrs. Lincoln's veil, $210

Handwritten letter, signed, by Lincoln to Major Ramsay
   about a lady who has two sons who *want* to work,
   $2,000

The Barrett sale established the knocking down of Old Abe
as big business. Lincoln stock shot up in the antique stores
and the rare-book shops. Avid collectors were transformed
into sniffing ferrets who haunted the galleries in search of
"sleepers"—rare relics, photographs, books, anything about
Lincoln that had escaped the vigilance of the auctioneer.

The action got hot in the auction galleries. Often when a
Lincoln relic was the prize a fencing match between bidders
would turn into a battle with broadswords. I've seen collectors scream and shout at each other and at the auctioneer in
their zeal to acquire a precious Lincoln souvenir.

On October 25, 1967, I put on the block at the Waldorf-
Astoria the great collection of Lincolniana assembled over
many years by Justin G. Turner of Los Angeles. The prices
fetched marked a mighty increase over those of the Barrett
sale a decade and a half earlier. Turner had acquired some of
the Barrett treasures and he and I watched with amazement as
wild bidders fought for them, forcing the prices up many

times above what they'd been only fifteen years earlier. Here are some of the records set at the Turner sale:

Page from Lincoln's sum book, $8,000

Franking signature of Lincoln as postmaster of New Salem, Illinois, $4,250

Copy of Lincoln's book on the debates with Douglas, inscribed by Lincoln to his former law partner, Stephen T. Logan, $8,500

Small wooden and cowhide trunk belonging to the Lincolns, $675

Lincoln's last letter, written on the day of his murder, April 14, 1865. Sold at Hamilton Galleries, 1967, $6,000

Office U. S. Military Telegraph.
WAR DEPARTMENT.

The following Telegram received at Washington, *11 P* M. *Apr 14* 1865

From Lexington Ky Apr 14 1865

Dr J. B. Todd

Care Col Vincent.

All goes well but you are missed. Geo H. Kinnear

The above telegram, sent to Dr. Todd by George H. Kinnear, his First Assistant in the Post Office at Lexington, Ky., arrived in Washington a few minutes after Abraham Lincoln was shot. Next day, at the postmortem, when a lock of hair, clipped from near the President's left temple, was given to Dr. Todd — finding no other paper in his pocket — he wrapped the lock, stained with blood or brain fluid, in this telegram and hastily wrote on it in pencil: "Hair of A. Lincoln."

J. A. T.

Bloody hair from Lincoln's head. Sold at Hamilton Galleries, 1967, $1,200

Partly printed check for $5 made out to "Tad when he is well enough to present," $5,500

The great seal of the President of the United States, $12,000 (Sold for $650 at the Barrett sale)

The Thirteenth Amendment on parchment, signed by Lincoln and others, $9,000 (Not the same as Barrett copy)

Lincoln's last letter, April 14, 1865, to the Commissioner of Indian Affairs, $6,000

Mrs. Lincoln's veil, $1,100 (Sold for $210 at the Barrett sale)

Blood-stained lock of Lincoln's hair, $1,200

Blood-stained portion of Lincoln's collar, removed after
  he was shot, $1,900

Printed reward broadside for Lincoln's murderers, April
  20, 1865, $800

Piece of soiled bandage used on Lincoln, $525

Metal spur with leather strap, believed to be Booth's,
  $725

Tiny fragment of black crepe from Lincoln's casket, $575

In the spring of 1978 the first part of the great collection of
Philip D. Sang of Chicago, rich in Lincolniana, was put up
for sale at Sotheby Parke Bernet and again prices leaped to
new highs. Here are a few outstanding records from the four
sessions of the Sang sale:

Handwritten Lincoln letter containing a manuscript poem
  by him, April 18, 1846, $31,000

Handwritten letter, signed, to Major Ramsay, $30,000
  (Sold for $2,000 at the Barrett sale)

Handwritten quotation signed by Lincoln about the
  Emancipation Proclamation, 1863, $14,000

Fragment of Lincoln's Annual Message to Congress, 11
  lines in Lincoln's hand, 1864, $5,000

Metal manacles used to secure Lincoln conspirator, Lewis
  Payne, $2,100 (I sold these privately in the late
  1950's for $150)

Reward poster for Lincoln's assassins. Sold at Hamilton Galleries, 1967, ➤
$800. When the owner displayed it in the window of a New York shop
in 1965, a spectator paused to look at it, then said: "Gosh! Are they
still looking for those guys?"

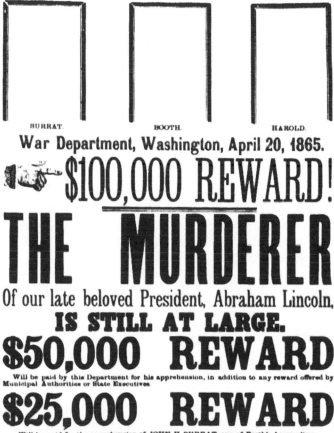

SURRAT.   BOOTH.   HAROLD.

War Department, Washington, April 20, 1865.

$100,000 REWARD!

THE MURDERER

Of our late beloved President, Abraham Lincoln,

IS STILL AT LARGE.

$50,000 REWARD

Will be paid by this Department for his apprehension, in addition to any reward offered by
Municipal Authorities or State Executives.

$25,000 REWARD

Will be paid for the apprehension of JOHN H. SURRAT, one of Booth's Accomplices.

$25,000 REWARD

Will be paid for the apprehension of David C. Harold, another of Booth's accomplices.

LIBERAL REWARDS will be paid for any information that shall conduce to the arrest of either of the above-
named criminals, or their accomplices.

All persons harboring or secreting the said persons, or either of them, or aiding or assisting their concealment or
escape, will be treated as accomplices in the murder of the President and the attempted assassination of the Secretary of
State, and shall be subject to trial before a Military Commission and the punishment of DEATH.

Let the stain of innocent blood be removed from the land by the arrest and punishment of the murderers.

All good citizens are exhorted to aid public justice on this occasion. Every man should consider his own conscience
charged with this solemn duty, and rest neither night nor day until it be accomplished.

EDWIN M. STANTON, Secretary of War.

DESCRIPTIONS.—BOOTH is Five Feet 7 or 8 inches high, slender build, high forehead, black hair, black eyes, and
wore a heavy black moustache, which there is some reason to believe has been shaved off.

JOHN H. SURRAT is about 5 feet, 9 inches. Hair rather thin and dark; eyes rather light; no beard. Would
weigh 145 or 150 pounds. Complexion rather pale and clear, with color in his cheeks. Wore light clothes of fine
quality. Shoulders square; cheek bones rather prominent; chin narrow; ears projecting at the top; forehead rather
low and square, but broad. Parts his hair on the right side; neck rather long. His lips are firmly set. A slim man.

DAVID C. HAROLD is five feet six inches high, hair dark, eyes dark, eyebrows rather heavy, full face, nose short,
hand short and fleshy, feet small, instep high, round bodied, naturally quick and active, slightly closes his eyes when
looking at a person.

NOTICE.—In addition to the above, State and other authorities have offered rewards amounting to almost one hundred thousand dollars, making an aggregate of about TWO HUNDRED THOUSAND DOLLARS.

Manacles used on Lewis Payne, Lincoln conspirator.
Sold at Sotheby Parke Bernet, 1978, $2,100

Handwritten letter from Lincoln to Grant, asking Grant
  to take care of Lincoln's son, Robert, who wished to
  join the army, $32,000

The Thirteenth Amendment, signed by Lincoln and
  others, $30,000 (Not the same as the Barrett and
  Turner copies)

Lincoln letter about the Emancipation Proclamation, July
  31, 1863, $13,500

The wild, upward spiral of prices continued at the Roy P.
Crocker sale held at Sotheby Parke Bernet on November 28,
1979. Here are a few of the notable records:

Printed check of Lincoln's filled out to "Tad,"
  Washington, 1861, $12,000

Handwritten letter signed to General Meade about a "rag-
  picker," $4,000

The Thirteenth Amendment, signed by Lincoln and
  others, $35,000 (Sold for $4,400 at the Barrett sale)

Printed reward broadside for Lincoln's murderers, $5,750
  (A similar broadside fetched $800 at the Turner
  sale)

Carved stone with betrothal of Lincoln and Ann
   Rutledge (the fake that fooled Sandburg), not
   warranted genuine by Sotheby Parke Bernet, $400

Glass pocket flask, engraved with Lincoln's name
   (Lincoln was a teetotaler), $3,000

Pen-holder, with pens and pencil, said to be Lincoln's,
   $1,700

Fragment of wallpaper from Lincoln's bedroom in
   Springfield, $325

Pair of black enamel opera glasses, said to be Lincoln's,
   $24,000

Beaverskin stovepipe hat, said to be Lincoln's, $10,000

Small compote, with cover, of White House china used
   during Lincoln's administration, $2,100

Mohair lap rug, said to be Lincoln's, $400

Blue military coat of the Black Hawk War period (1833),
   said to be Lincoln's when a captain, $2,000

Highest priced of all Lincoln mementoes are his original
letters and papers and the letters of those who loved or hated
him. In 1949 a two-page manuscript copy, written and signed
by Lincoln, of his "Gettysburg Address" was sold for $54,000
at Parke-Bernet Galleries to a Cuban millionaire. It was the
greatest bargain of the century. Old Hyman Parke, president
of the great gallery, then an American institution, wept at
the fall of the ivory hammer, for he had expected this famed
historic speech to fetch at least $100,000. I will take a blood
oath on a split-rail fence that if that same two-page message
in Lincoln's hand were put on the block today it would fetch
a million dollars.

I've sold hundreds, perhaps thousands, of Lincoln letters and documents at auction, but the one I loved most (and on the sale of which I didn't make a cent) was the note that Lincoln wrote to twelve-year-old Grace Bedell who suggested that he grow a beard. That exciting fragment of Americana passed into the collection of David L. Wolper, the Hollywood producer, at the modest price of $20,000. I won't even venture a guess at its value today.

Most voraciously sought of Lincoln notes are those in which he pardoned youthful soldiers for desertion or falling asleep at their posts. Usually Lincoln issued such pardons at the risk of irritating his hot-tempered secretary of war, Edwin M. Stanton who, in sheer pique at Lincoln's unprofessional magnanimity, dubbed Abe "that long-armed baboon in the White House." To appease Stanton, Lincoln learned to skirt the term *pardon*. He merely suspended the execution "until further orders." One tearful mother said to Lincoln: "But that means my boy may still be shot."

Lincoln pardons a deserter. Handwritten telegram from Lincoln to General Meade, ordering a sentence of death suspended "until further orders." Sold at Hamilton Galleries, 1970, $1,000

"If your son lives until further orders from me," said Abe, putting his arm over her shoulder, "he'll live to be as old as ten Methuselahs piled on top of each other."

The craze for Lincoln relics has spurred forgers to create fresh goods for the auction market. Even those who knew Lincoln contributed to the supply of fakes. The half-batty Mary Todd Lincoln complained not long after Abe was murdered: "I enclose a very few hairs from my beloved husband's head. I regret I have so few to spare you as I have only a bunch as large as one of your fingers."

Despite her lamentably small supply of Lincoln's hair right after his death, Mary continued for many years to pass out locks profligately, all authenticated in her own hand. She also possessed an inexhaustible supply of Lincoln's canes.

The Barrett sale offered the usual spate of historic frauds. In my book, *Great Forgers and Famous Fakes* (1980), I discussed twelve forgers of Lincolniana and alluded to several of Barrett's notorious relics:

> Most delightful and harmless of all Lincoln forgeries are the relics "dug up" on the site of New Salem, Illinois, about twenty miles from Springfield, where Lincoln spent four years of his young manhood. There from the earth were exhumed the grub hoe used by young Lincoln, his ox yoke, an ax helve carved with the rail-splitter's name, and a flat rock "discovered" by one William Green, on which is incised, "A. Lincoln and Ann Rutledge were betrothed here July 4, 1833."
>
> What is appealing about these spurious relics is that they found their way into the collection of Oliver R. Barrett, noted Lincoln buff, and thence into the biography of Lincoln by Carl Sandburg. The poet who immortalized Chicago and fog and cool tombs was willing to suspend his critical acumen to admit these romantic

fakes into his biography of the emancipator. The fron-
tispiece to the first volume of Sandburg's work was the ax
helve (which the big-city poet called an ax *handle*), a
piece of wood bearing Abe's jackknife signature that had
miraculously defied the corrosive effect of earth and
dampness for over one hundred years. But the gem of the
collection, also illustrated by Sandburg, was the flat stone
recording what was almost certainly a mythical
engagement between Lincoln and Ann Rutledge. The
whole tale of this frontier love between Abe and Ann
rests upon the tenuous word of Lincoln's law partner and
biographer, William H. Herndon. In July, 1833, Ann
Rutledge was probably still engaged to one John McNeil.
But the movies, and the Chicago poets, Sandburg and
Masters, have wrought a beautiful American legend of
the alleged love between Lincoln and the little New
Salem girl who died in 1835—"Bloom forever, O
Republic, from the dust of my bosom."

Less obvious fakes that plague every collector and cling like
fungus on the pages of history are the Lincoln letters forged
by Joseph Cosey, Charles "the Baron" Weisberg, and Eugene
Field II. They often crop up in small-town auctions and at big
New York sales when the expertise is remiss. The collector
should especially be wary of any books or pamphlets supposedly signed by Lincoln. I've seen such impostors knocked
down for huge sums to unsuspecting collectors or historians.

The most skilled of this nefarious trio was Weisberg who
often tacked forged endorsements on authentic documents. A
begging letter to Lincoln, of which thousands were dispatched that never got to the president's desk, has but a
trifling value. But under the magic of Weisberg's pen these
nigh-worthless papers are enlivened with a pithy note in
Lincoln's familiar script. I was once fooled by such a

document. I had examined it rather hastily and okayed it for inclusion in one of my early auctions. Not until I saw it printed in facsimile in the catalog, where its deficiencies were more obvious, did I discover the blunder, fortunately in time to prevent its sale. I kept my discovery and my embarrassment to myself. Unobtrusively and with the silent stealth of a footpad I whisked the interloper away into my private collection of forgeries.

On another occasion, in the fall of 1974, I was less fortunate. I offered for sale an antique shaving mirror "used by Abraham Lincoln." It was accompanied, as usual with fakes, by a lengthy authentication that had about it the ring of truth: "I certify that the three-piece French mirror belonged to Lincoln and was in Lincoln's family many years. . . . My husband had it given to him 50 yrs. ago. The mirror was in Lincoln's home many years." This relic was knocked down to Ralph Newman of the Abraham Lincoln Bookshop in Chicago. Newman kept it a few weeks and after a lot of research discovered that the mirror was of a type and design not in use during Lincoln's lifetime. I refunded Ralph's money at once.

Sometimes relics of Lincoln turn up that are very suspect. In November, 1979, as noted in my list of items at the Crocker sale, a pair of opera glasses supposedly used by Lincoln on the night of his murder sold for $24,000. They were accompanied by an affidavit stating that Captain James M. McCamly, of the Washington City guard, had discovered them on the floor of Lincoln's box. There are, however, some very cogent reasons to put a big question mark after the claim that these glasses belonged to Lincoln:

1. They were cheap, rather ugly opera glasses, worth perhaps $5, and certainly not the sort of glasses that the President of the United States would take to a theater. Virtually all of Lincoln's possessions as president were costly

Are these Lincoln's opera glasses? Allegedly used by Lincoln on the night of his murder, April 14, 1865. Sold at Sotheby Parke Bernet, 1979, $24,000

and beautiful, many of them gifts from his admirers.

2. Lincoln had previously visited the presidential box at Ford's Theatre. He was aware that it overhung the stage, only twelve feet up, and that he would be almost close enough to touch the actors. If he'd leaned out of the box with opera glasses he might have banged Laura Keene on the head. Why, then, would he lug along to the opera a pair of cheap, useless opera glasses?

3. From the moment the shot of the assassin exploded in the theater, as I have pointed out, the flag-draped box was invaded by a jostling horde who carried out the dying president and then tore the box to pieces in a quest for souvenirs. During the struggle, no doubt, one of the relic hunters dropped his opera glasses, found later by Captain McCamly. Someone else picked up the case for the glasses and later presented it to the Ford's Theatre Museum.

4. Nor do I believe that the opera glasses belonged to

Major Henry R. Rathbone who was in the box with the president on the night of the murder. Major Rathbone would not have carried a pair of cheap opera glasses to a performance where he would sit almost within touching distance of the actors.

At the same sale was sold for $10,000 a stovepipe hat with a Springfield label that allegedly belonged to Honest Abe. One historian, shaking his head, complained to me: "That hat had everything going for it. It was the kind of hat Lincoln sometimes wore. It came from his home town. It was probably made in the late 1850s, when Lincoln was living in Springfield.

"The only trouble is that it wasn't Lincoln's size!"

CHAPTER 8

My Clashes with the FBI

THE OLD FBI was a mighty scary outfit. Its secret agents, impeccably attired and deceptively polite, were everywhere, bugging offices, tapping telephones, keeping "lists," chasing crooks, and, now and then, just for the ducks of it, harrassing honest citizens.

It was this Nazi-like FBI, the J. Edgar Hoover gang, that roused my ire and with whom I clashed.

And always over a few old papers I put up at auction!

In those days, nearly two decades ago when my auction gallery was new, I was inspired by the spirit of adventure. Nothing daunted me. I greeted with enthusiasm my fellow soldiers who had served in Europe during World War II. I'd reminisce with them while they displayed their war souvenirs—documents of Hitler and Goering, Nazi medals, and other relics.

"I've got something here that I think will interest you," said one craggy old fellow, obviously a survivor of many campaigns. He handed me a small, elaborately bound volume. "The morning after I picked up this little souvenir our outfit got nailed by an artillery barrage. My best friend got killed."

I opened the book. A quick look revealed a large collection of intimate, handwritten letters of Frederick the Great.

I fixed a sharp eye on my visitor and asked: "Out of what museum did you steal this little book?"

"What do you mean?" His face whitened.

"Exactly what I said."

"Well," he explained, "I was with General Patton when we crossed into Germany. Ike didn't let us go as fast as we wanted to, so naturally the devil found an amusement for us. We put our spare time to use in driving our tanks into buildings that were still standing and we picked up some great war souvenirs.

"Patton, as you know, collected old pistols and he got most of his collection right out of German museums. We only did what he did. Ran our tanks into the walls of libraries and museums. It was easier than going in through the door.

"I don't even remember the name of the library where I got this book, or even the town it was in. My mind is like a big pile of rubble. Smashed-up bricks and smashed-up bodies is about all I remember." He paused. "Can you sell the book for me?"

"Sure," I said. "I'm always delighted to profit from anything stolen out of Nazi Germany. I look at it this way. The Nazis wanted a fight. They got a fight. And if you start a fight and lose it, why there's always a penalty to pay."

The collection of thirty-two letters by the great Prussian ruler, Frederick II, was worth several thousand dollars. I described it in detail for my auction catalog. But even before it got into print I received a visit from two handsome young men neatly attired in conservative business suits. They flashed their badges and ID cards with that neat flip of the wrist that marks the well-trained FBI man. I glanced at their photographs.

"What can I do for you, gentlemen?" I asked.

"We'll come right to the point, Mr. Hamilton," said one. "We've had a complaint from the German consul in Washington that you're offering for sale a collection of letters of Frederick the Great, stolen from one of the big German libraries during the war. The consul has asked us to pick up these letters and turn them over to him, as they are a part of the national heritage of Germany."

"Your summary of the situation is quite correct," I said. "But are you certain you want to take these letters away from me? You know, the Germans aren't giving us back the Americans who died to get them."

"The point is, Mr. Hamilton," said the spokesman for the two agents, "you are offering for sale stolen letters and we are here now, politely asking that you assist us in returning them to the rightful owners."

"Then I shall do as you ask. I'll have the letters here in my office promptly at ten o'clock tomorrow morning."

"Very good, sir," said the spokesman. "We'll see you at ten." We shook hands.

As the two men reached the door, I said, seemingly as an afterthought: "Oh, by the way, be sure to wear blue shirts for the television cameras."

"What television cameras?"

"Well, you know, what you're about to do is newsworthy. I'm sure all the TV stations will want to cover the story. I think the American people will be interested to learn that the FBI is now working for the German government."

Later that day the FBI called to say that they wouldn't be around to pick up the letters of Frederick the Great, and I sold them as scheduled.

On another occasion my skirmish with the FBI was more ferocious. On June 4, 1965, I got a letter from Evelyn Fagan of Maryland, wife of a former chief radioman in the United States Navy. She offered for auction a log of the Seventh Fleet Communication Station that recorded all the messages, many of them in code, sent and received between General MacArthur and the Japanese high command leading up to the surrender of the Japanese forces on the battleship

"Missouri." The log had been brought home as a souvenir by Chief Radioman Gerald B. Fagan. An exciting relic, undoubtedly fished out of the wastebasket! I accepted the twenty-two yellowing pages and cataloged them for sale on September 30, 1965:

JAPANESE SURRENDER. The original 7th Fleet Communications log, 31 full pages, folio and 2½ full pages, 4 to, August 14-18, 1945 . . . (400.00)

Amazing historical document, the original typed communications log kept by U.S. Navy personnel attached to Commander, 7th Fleet, the station through which all communications passed to and from ships at sea and Allied Headquarters of General MacArthur in Manila. The messages are in their original state, many slightly garbled and in code, and mostly on official mimeographed "Radio Log Sheets," with the circuit (some on "Tokio Intercept") frequency, and with names of operators and supervisors. This log furnishes a first-hand account of Allied surrender negotiations with Japan: "From Supreme Commander for the Allied Powers to Japanese General Headquarters: Your messages of August sixteenth numbers one and two have been received and are satisfactory . . . every possible precaution will be taken to insure the safety of the planes bearing the Japanese representatives on their mission . . . type of plane to be your Navy Type Zero Model twenty-two, three, or your Army type one naught naught transport plane KI five seven . . .

"From the Japanese GHQ to the Allied Supreme Commander BT No. 3 August 16, or about noon a group of some twelve Allied transports approached extremely near the coast of Kochi Shikoku. At that time the

Imperial order to cease hostilities had not yet been issued
and our air units ventured to attack . . . causing some
damage.

"The Supreme Commander of the Allied Powers
further directs the Japanese Imperial Government to send
to his headquarters at Manila a competent representative
impowered to receive certain requirements for carrying
into effect the terms of surrender . . ."

A fascinating political analysis discusses contingencies
"if Soviets had remained neutral or if atomic bombs had
not been employed against Japan." The log also includes
the full text of the Japanese Emperor's message of
surrender.

Exciting, important record of the conclusion of World
War II, in fine condition.

The publication of the catalog brought two young Naval
Intelligence officers to my gallery. They were pleasant and
polite, and it was hard to refuse their request that I turn over
to them the Fagan papers.

I explained: "I'm sure you will agree that these historical
records survived only because of the foresight of the chief
radioman who brought them back to America. Your contention that they were illegally removed from naval archives I
find untenable. However, if you can furnish me with
evidence that you have a few similar documents of the same
period to establish that these were taken out of sequence I'll
turn over what I have to you. But I suspect that you have no
other documents at all of this era and now wish to seize these
without even compensating the owner."

After an exchange of chilly pleasantries, the two officers
walked out. They were back in a few hours.

"May we borrow the file and photograph it for our
records?"

DATE_____ COMMANDER SEVENTH FLEET OPERATOR _____
                      COMMUNICATIONS
PAGE_____   RADIO LOG SHEET   CIRCUIT_____

SUPVR _____   FREQ. _____

GCT	ALL ENTRIES ARE TO BE MADE IN ACCORDANCE WITH COMINST.
BE	UPON THE SIDES OF THE FUSELAGE AND TOP AND BOTTOM OF EACH WING GREEN CROSSES EASILY VISIBLE AT 5ØØ YARDS STOP THE AIRPLANE WILL BE CAPABLE OF INFLIGHT VOICE COMMUNICATIONS COMMA IN ENGLISH COMMA ON A FREQUENCY OF 697Ø KCS STOP AIRPLANE WILL PROFI TO AN AIRFIELON THE ISLAND OF IE SHIMA COMMA IDENTI IDENTIFIED BY 2 WHITE CROSSES PROMINENTLY IN THE CENTER OF THE RUNWAY STOP THE EXACT DATE OF HOUR THE AIRPLANE WILL DEPART FROM SATA MISAKI COMMA ON T E SOUTHERN TIP OF KYUSHU COMMA THE ROUTE AND ALTITUDE OF FLIGHT AND ESTIMATED TH OF ARRIVAL IN IE SHIMA COMMA WILL BE KNKNKN IN ADVANCE COMMA IN ENGLISH COMMA FROM TOKYO ON A FEQENCY OF 16125 KCS STOP ACKNO' LEDGEMENT BY THA FROM THES HEADQUARTERS TER OF THE RECEIPT OF SUCS BROADCAST IS REQUIRED PRIOR TO TAKE DASH OFF KK OF THE AIRPLANE STOP WEATHER PERMITTING COMMA THE AIRPLAN WILL DEPART FROM SATA MISATKI BETWEEN HOURSOF Ø8ØØ AND 11ØØ TOKYO TIME ON THE 17 THE DAY OF AUGUST 1945 STOP IN COMMUNICATIO REGARDING THES FLIGHT COMMA THE CODE DESIGNATED QUOTE BATAAN UNQUOTE WILL BE EMPLOYED PARA THE AIRPLA E WILL APPROACH IE SHIM ON A COURSE OF 18Ø DEGREES AND CIRCLE LANDING FIELD AT 1ØØØ FEET OR BELOW THE CLOUD LAYER UNTIL METBY AN ESCORT OF UNQTED STATES P DASH THIRTY 38 S WHICH WILL LEAD IT TO A LANDING STOP SUCH ESCORT MAY JOIN THE AIRPLANE PRIOR TO R AT IE SHIMA BT MACAURTHER
Ø22Ø	
	THE S COMMANDER FOR POWERS IS TO BE N WONCE OF THE EFFECTIVE DAY OF SUCH CEISHAT OF HOVE COMMA WHERE UPON ALLIED FORCES WILL BE RERC O CEASE HOSTILITIE SUPREMA COMMA OF THE ALLIED POR FULE DIRECTE PHILIPPINE ISLINDS THE EMPEROR OF JAPIN THOMMAT CERTAIN REQUIRE MENTS FOR CIRRYING I THE TERMSOF SURREND EF SEOF THE ABOVE REPRESE WA REPRESENTIVES WALL PRESENT E COMMANDER FOR THE ILLIED POWERS UPON HIS ARRIVIL ADOKEUENT AUTH PIRA THE REPRESENTATIVE WILL HE ACCOMPINIED BY COMPETENT ABVISO RS REPRESNTIG THE JAPANESE ARMY COMMA THE JAPANESE NAVY AND THE JAPANESE AIR RORCES E HOP THE BATTER ADVISOR WILL THE FIMILIAR WHTH FICILIT IN THE TOKYO PROCEDSRE FOR TRINSPORT OF THE IBOVE PARTEY STELR SAFE CONDUCT IS PREV OF COMMA FROM WHICH POINT THEY WILL THE TRANSPORTED TO MIALA TROMMA PHILIPPINE ISLI D S COMMA FA STATES AIRPBINE VOPTHEY WILL HE REURNED EO JAPAN IN THE SAME MANNER WILL EMPLYY AN UNARMED AIRPLI COMA TYPE MODER 22 FOMMA L 2 COMMA D 3 SICH AIRPLINE TILL THE PAINTD ALL WHITE AND WILL THAE UPON THE SIDESOF THE FUSELAGE AND TOP AND THOMTTOM OF EICH UING GBEEN CROSHS EASILY RECOGNIZI AT HOP THE AIRPLAN WILL THE CAPABLE OF INFLIGHT VOICE COMUNICAT IONG COMMAI ENGLISH COMMA ON AFREQUENCY OF 697Ø KCS HOP AIRPLANE WILL PROCEED TO IN AIRDROME ON THE AISLAND OF IE SHIMACOMMA INDTUI BY 2 PHITE PROM INENTLY DISPLATWED IN THE CENTER THE RSNWIT HOR THE EXICT DATE AND HOUR THIS AARPLANE WILL DEPART FROM SATA MISAKI COMMA ON THE SOUTHERN TIP OF KYUSHUCOMA THE ROUET ARE OF ELIGHT AND ESTIUME D TIME OF ARRIVIL IN EE COMMA WAFROM TOKYO ON A FREQUENCY OF 16125 THE RECEIPT OF S CH BROADCAST IS REQUIRED PRIORTO TAKE DASH OFF OFTHE AIRPLANE VOP PERMITTING CO AIRPLANE WELLDEP AIR DEPART FROM SATA MISAKI BETWEEN THE SOURS OF Ø8ØØ AND 12ØØ TOKYO TIME ON THE 17 TH DIY OF AUGUST 1945 SOP IN TROMMUNICATIO NS REGARDING THIS FLIGHT COMMA THE CODE DESIGNATION QUOTE BATAAN UNQUOTE BATAAN UN QUOTE WILL BE EMPLOYED PARA THE AIRPLANE WILL IPP RACH ON A COURSE OF 18Ø DE GREES AND CIRCLE LINDING F I ELD AT 18ØØ 1ØØØ FEET OR BELO CLOUL UNTIL JONE ZY AN ESCORT OF ANITED VATES ARMY DASH 3 P 38S WHICH WILL LE IT TO A LANDING HOP SUCH FVORT MAY JOIN THE AIRPLANE

Rare document claimed by the FBI and the Navy Department. Original Teletype message received by Seventh Fleet Communications about the Japanese surrender to MacArthur, 1945

"Certainly," I said.

They took the file, photographed it, and returned it.

The next day marked the inevitable arrival of two FBI men. They were good-looking, outwardly affable, and intent upon taking the Fagan file away with them.

"Admiral Eller is eager to add these papers to the naval archives and he cannot understand why you persist in refusing to return them to the authorities in Washington."

I again explained my position.

"I am sure," said one of the FBI agents, "if you will put us in touch with the owner he will be happy to see these historic papers placed in the naval archives."

The FBI men asked for the name and address of the consignor.

I picked up the telephone and called my attorney who said: "Whenever the ownership of a document is in question, the name of the consignor must cease to be confidential."

I gave the FBI the information they wanted.

The next morning Mrs. Fagan telephoned me. She was hysterical. "The man from the FBI threatened us," she said, sobbing. "He said he'd get my husband fired from his job if we didn't sign over to the navy all the radio messages."

"Don't worry," I told her.

That afternoon I got a telegram from her husband, Gerald R. Fagan: "Remove from any auction papers forwarded to you by Mrs. Evelyn M. Fagan and return to me the owner."

It was Mr. Fagan's right, I judged, to give in to bullies. But there was no obligation for me to do it, so I just held on to the papers. Then came a second communication, this one a carbon of a letter Mrs. Fagan had written on October 5, 1965, to Rear Admiral Eller, Office of the Chief of Naval Operations in Washington:

"It is our desire that the documents now being held by Charles Hamilton, Autographs Inc. . . . be delivered to you by Mr. Hamilton upon receipt of this letter . . . I Gerald B. Fagan and I Evelyn M. Fagan relinquish all claim to the above documents, to become the property of the United States Navy."

I asked our vice president, H. Keith Thompson, Jr., who himself had served brilliantly as a naval officer in Admiral Byrd's last Antarctic expedition, to help me draft a reply. Together we prepared and sent the following answer to Mr. Fagan, with copies to Admiral Eller and the FBI:

"Your communication of October 5th has been received.

"We will be pleased to hand over your property to Admiral Eller or his authorized agent at an agreed time if he will call for it here. The presentation will take place in front of TV cameras and in the presence of newsmen, for we feel it in the national interest that the American people be informed as to the role of the Office of Naval Intelligence and the Federal Bureau of Investigation in the forced acquest of private property."

In threatening to have Mr. Fagan discharged from his job the FBI had overreached itself and I knew it. They knew it, too. I never heard from them or from the navy again. And that is why these old papers are still in my files. They aren't mine, and Mr. Fagan has formally relinquished his ownership. And so, one of these days when I simmer down a bit I'll pack them up and send them to the Naval Archives in Washington.

CHAPTER 9

The Purloined Parchment

SCORES OF EXCITING tales could be told about nearly every old document or painting, tales of sordid barter, theft, and greed. Such stories are seldom set on paper. They might implicate personages in high places or embarrass innocent people. But here is one tale that can now be told, since two members of the cast are dead and the third, once a notorious thief, is now giving a wide berth to the primrose path.

In the summer of 1958 a close acquaintance of mine, widely known as a skilled antiquarian famed for uncovering rarities, drifted into my office and settled his arachnidan frame into a chair opposite my desk.

"I've located something great for you," he said. "It belongs to a mildewy historical society in New Jersey. They're strapped for cash and I think they'll tumble if I wave a grand under their noses."

"What's the item?"

"You'll see," he said. "You've got a customer for top constitutional stuff, haven't you?"

I nodded. I was thinking of the noted Chicago collector, Philip D. Sang, to whom I'd sold dozens of superb documents about the writing and interpretation of the United States Constitution. Sang's collection was rich in letters of the founding fathers, intimate letters recording their aspirations and hopes for the success of the new nation.

"If all goes well," my friend went on, "I shall place in your hands tomorrow an old parchment that will really put some voltage in your corpuscles."

The document he laid before me the next day was a creamy white roll of crackling parchment that looked like a telescope of sheep's skin. As I unrolled it I saw engrossed in huge, ornate script the immortal words: "We the People of the United States in order to form a more perfect union. . . ." A fervor of mingled excitement and joy and patriotism swept over me as I fondled the precious parchment, actually the original ratification of the United States Constitution by the State of New Jersey. It was penned on two enormous sheets in a fine, flowing script and bore the signatures of more than a score of American patriots including John Witherspoon and Richard Stockton, both of whom had also signed the Declaration of Independence.

In a few moments the document was mine at the astonishingly low price of $1,500, the precise sum asked by the lanky antiquarian.

After my visitor walked out with my check, I quietly closed the door to my office, shutting out the inquisitive eyes of my secretaries. Then I cradled the rare old vellum relic in my arms and exulted over my purchase.

But that very afternoon I offered it to Phil Sang at exactly double what I'd paid. He jumped at the chance to add it to his collection and mailed me a batch of postdated checks, his customary form of remittance, to cover the purchase.

A few months later I discovered that the antiquarian who sold me the document was a thief. He had systematically looted the archives of Philadelphia and possibly even New Jersey. As a result of my testimony he was arrested and sentenced to prison for stealing historic papers. Since he has long ago resigned his membership in the light-fingered gentry it would serve no purpose to reveal his name.

But after his arrest I kicked around in my mind the thought

that perhaps he had snitched the old parchment from some venerable government archive, possibly even from Rutgers, the state university, where many historic treasures are preserved.

If he'd stolen the parchment I'd find out fast enough, for Sang was proud of his great collection and often placed large parts of it on display throughout the nation.

My new autograph auction was now flourishing and I secretly hoped that Sang would let me sell on his behalf a few of the prize items that I'd uncovered for him. Several years passed and I continued to hope that one day the telephone would ring (Sang rarely transacted any business by mail) and the great collector would ask: "Can you give me the latest evaluation of the New Jersey ratification?"

And those were almost his exact words when he finally called my office asking for an appraisal of this cornerstone document of American history.

"I'm going to give it away," Sang explained, "and I need an evaluation for tax purposes."

I made a brief but unsuccessful effort to beguile him into selling it at auction.

"Very well," I said. "I'll appraise it for you at more than three times what you paid five years ago."

"Not exactly what I had in mind," said Sang.

"Since I sold it to you for $3,000, I don't feel I should go much over $10,000. Would your larcenous instincts be placated with an appraisal of $15,000?"

"I'll think about it."

Later that day I got a call from Professor David Randall of the Lilly Library in Indiana.

"Charles, I've been asked by Phil Sang to appraise the New Jersey ratification of the Constitution. He tells me he bought it from you. What's it worth?"

I briefed Dave.

"It sounds to me like a $25,000 document," he said. "Greatest constitutional item I ever heard of. I think you've undervalued it."

Another day went by. The phone rang and it was Dave. "Phil got the appraisal he was looking for, not from me but from Dave Kirschenbaum—$50,000. Sang's going to present the document to Rutgers and they're giving him an honorary degree."

In only five years, the noble parchment had come full cycle. Witness the following "bill of particulars":

To antiquarian who "discovered" the parchment	$1,500.00
To Charles Hamilton, who sold it to Sang	1,500.00
To David Kirschenbaum of the Carnegie Book Shop, who appraised it, approximately	500.00
To Philip D. Sang, for tax deduction	50,000.00
To Philip D. Sang, an honorary degree, monetary value, about	10,000.00
	$63,500.00

If these figures are not enough to prove that crime sometimes pays handsomely, with no harm done, consider this: During its sabbatical the old document was tenderly handled and loved, increased greatly in monetary value, and, through the attention lavished on it by manuscript experts and collectors, attained a fresh and exalted status at Rutgers, thus forever ensuring its careful preservation and protection against thieves and marauders.

CHAPTER 10

Basil Rathbone's Last Adventure

I'VE HEARD Jackie Onassis called selfish, even by her close personal friends. I've heard her called greedy. I've heard her called unkind. And I know that her opinion of me is that I'm an invidious rascal bent on making a buck out of invading her privacy.

A lot of people, I guess, share this last opinion and I'm not going to defend myself. But I want to say that I agree with Basil Rathbone's description of Jackie as "a great lady." Rathbone never fully realized why his remark was so true and I never told him. Only now can I relate all the facts about what took place fifteen years ago when the noted actor consigned to me for public sale a little packet of letters written to him by Jackie.

When I first met Rathbone he was 71, but he looked as if he had just stepped out of one of Conan Doyle's Holmes stories. He was tall and handsome, impeccably dressed, with a sharp, twinkling eye that flashed like a Toledo rapier. He had a rich voice of pure gold. There was an awesome severity in his appearance that momentarily, but only momentarily, hid the warmth of his personality. For Rathbone was at heart a sentimentalist, a romantic through and through. In another time and place he might have been a courtier, a poet, or perhaps a gallant prince and patron of the arts. Basil was prodigal with his love for people and things. He had spent his life in stintless giving, and now in the twilight of his great career he was broke. I sensed the lamentable state of his affairs the moment he sat down to lunch with Diane and me.

At first I strove to put our conversation on Sherlock Holmes, for I'd read and re-read many times all the fifty-odd tales in the sacred canon. But Rathbone would have none of such paltry discourse.

"The character of Holmes is not a very interesting one," he remarked. "It is an easy role to play, always the same. Holmes never changes.

"I was invited to join that club devoted to Sherlock Holmes, the Baker Street Irregulars. But I politely declined. I'd had enough of old Sherlock in the films."

I said: "You're ungrateful, Mr. Rathbone. You owe your great fame to Sherlock Holmes."

Rathbone acknowledged my praise with a little smile and said: "For that compliment I shall recite a poem to you both. And he intoned in his beautiful voice a few verses about Holmes' adventures in London by gaslight.

"I never got a penny from the Holmes residuals," said Rathbone. "In the late 1930s, I think it was, when television was nothing but a wild dream, I sold the TV rights to all my films for $500 and I promptly lent the five hundred to a down-and-out actor who never repaid me."

By dessert, the conversation, during which Basil had chatted about his recent activities, was settled upon Shakespeare.

Rathbone and I talked fervently of the great dramatist, orchestrating our favorite passages from the famous and not-so-famous plays until at last Rathbone mentioned his real reason for lunching with us.

"I wanted to make sure you weren't just a merchant without a soul before entrusting to you my three wonderful letters from Jacqueline Kennedy. And from the moment you spoke so joyously of Shakespeare I knew you were the only person to handle their sale."

The letters that Basil turned over to me were truly superb missives, all penned in Mrs. Kennedy's fastidious script and full of the affection that she and the president felt for the genius of Shakespeare.

Rathbone agreed to write, in his own hand, a description of the historic reading in the White House that had inspired the letters, later to sell at auction for $1,600. Basil wrote several pages commenting on his astonishment and delight at being invited to perform and his further joy when he discovered that John F. Kennedy knew the St. Crispin speech from memory. "If I faltered in my recitation," he said, "there was the president standing by, ready to prompt me."

The letters from Jackie revealed her impeccable taste and gentle wit and showed her great consideration as first lady for the guests of the White House.

Perhaps the most exciting and touching letters ever penned by a first lady, this remarkable correspondence gives a wonderful insight into the thousand days of Camelot when Kennedy was president. Rathbone had been asked, with others, to recite for the president and other guests, including the Grand Duchess of Luxembourg. The program had already been planned but Rathbone suggested a change that inspired Mrs. Kennedy's first letter:

> Is it not funny how things become over complicated? I am sorry you thought the President "would accept no other" speech but St. Crispin. It is just one of his favorites for whatever lovely dreams of leading or being led on to victory lurk in his soul! He also knows it by heart and I suppose wanted it for the same selfish reasons I asked for so much Donne and other things I love. He also loves Henry V (and he reminds me of him—though I don't think he knows that!)
>
> However I agree completely with all your reasons for thinking the speech inappropriate—they had never

occurred to me—nor had the ones for the Richard II "farewell King" speech being so ideal. (I have not got it beside me. I just hope it has no line about Kings being despots that will make the poor Grand Duchess think everyone wants to push her off her throne!) If there is some insidious line you could leave it out. . . .

On the following day Mrs. Kennedy changed her mind and wrote:

I know you are against St. Crispin. It is because of delicacy of feeling. You are an Englishman. That was Agincourt. There are difficulties now between England and the continent. You are giving this speech as an Englishman at the White House before a European head of State. I think it is very sensitive of you to think of such things. But I made my husband read the speech aloud to me last night and told him of your reservations.

Shall I tell you why I think it is appropriate—he thinks so too but I cannot quote him adequately. Of all the speeches that make you care and want to make the extra effort—sacrifice, fight, or die—for whatever cause—that is the one. The only person I would not wish you to say it in front of was Khruschev, as we are not united in purpose . . . we are all striving for the same brave things today. . . . I promise I will not change my mind again if you will promise to do St. Crispin and forget about all the little hidden meanings in it. . . . Please say you agree.

Neither Basil nor I was prepared for the angry public reaction that saluted the appearance of the letters in my auction catalog. The front page of every daily in America carried the lurid headlines that Rathbone was selling private letters written to him by the wife of the martyred president. It was less than two years since Kennedy's murder and Jackie was still the sacrosanct goddess of the tabloids, inviolate and beyond reproach. Rathbone had "abused her confidence" and the grand old actor, impoverished and soon to die, was peppered with cheap shots by pen-and-ink snipers.

Rathbone was crushed. He telephoned me. "What have I done? What have I done, Charles? Have I really done something wicked?"

I tried to reassure him and calm him down. I urged him to meet with members of the press, but he refused: "I don't think I can face anyone right now."

Just when it seemed that the assaults on Rathbone were dying down, a new headline flashed across the nation, stunning the old actor, who was an avid admirer—I might say adorer—of the former first lady:

JACKIE UPSET BY PLAN TO SELL HER LETTERS

Mrs. Jacqueline Kennedy is deeply resentful over the impending auction of some of her personal letters, sources close to her said today.

Basil heard the news on the radio and called me. I could tell that he'd been and perhaps still was crying.

"Charles," he said, and his words came slowly between long pauses, "do you think the great lady really hates me now? Have I disgraced myself? Perhaps I should withdraw the letters from the sale. It's not too late, is it?"

"I doubt very much," I told him, "that Mrs. Kennedy disapproves of the sale. Her letters are so beautiful, wonderful mementoes of an historic occasion. Why should she be critical of their sale?"

"She's truly a great lady," said Rathbone. "Perhaps you're right."

Basil was so terribly upset that I feared for his health. I

decided to make an appeal direct to Jacqueline Kennedy. I wrote a letter addressed to her or to her secretary, Pamela Turnure, at 400 Park Avenue in New York where Mrs. Kennedy was then in residence. My letter revealed some very private information about Rathbone. I sent it by messenger and, as it was an intimate letter not to be viewed by any person other than the recipients, I kept no copy of it. But it ran like this:

VERY PERSONAL

Dear Mrs. Kennedy:

Mr. Rathbone is extremely distressed and depressed because he has read in the newspapers and heard over the radio that you disapprove of the sale of your letters to him.

Were he not strapped for money, I'm certain that Mr. Rathbone would never part with your letters, for he counts them among his greatest treasures. But he has very little income and earns only a meager living by recitals at schools and colleges for which he receives a fee of $100 per appearance, plus travel expenses.

Mr. Rathbone's daughter, Cynthia, has long been ill with hepatitis. With the money he receives from the sale of your letters, he hopes to take his daughter on a much needed vacation.

If you could find some way to deny the newspaper reports of your displeasure at the sale of the letters, I know that it would buoy Mr. Rathbone's spirits and make him a very happy man.

Only you and I must know that I wrote this letter.
                    Sincerely,

                    Charles Hamilton

Less than an hour after I dispatched the letter, Mrs. Turnure called a press conference at which she stated: "Mrs. Kennedy isn't even aware of the sale of her letters, as far as I know."

Basil heard the news over the radio and telephoned me, jubilant.

"You see, Charles, I was right," he told me. "Mrs. Kennedy is a great lady, a very great lady."

CHAPTER 11

The "Secret Reserve" System

NOT LONG AGO I was standing in the handsome art gallery on the third floor of Sotheby Parke Bernet on Madison Avenue, admiring the beautiful paintings that were soon to ornament new walls. I was so enwrapped in the glory of the Renaissance that I did not notice a little old lady near me until I heard a peevish voice in my ear: "What irks me about most auction sales is that they really aren't auction sales at all."

"What do you mean?" I asked.

My new acquaintance seemed on the verge of shaking up a few podiums and I listened attentively as she continued: "Take this sale, for instance," and she moved her slender arm in a dramatic arc to encompass most of the paintings on the walls. "Every single painting here is already priced, either by the owner or by the gallery. Most of the prices are high retail figures, as much as you'd pay in a fancy art shop.

"I know the gentleman who consigned these paintings and he has no intention of letting them go for a cent less than their top value. He assembled this collection just to make money and he is determined to get a profit or take his merchandise home with him."

I urged the old lady to continue.

"Everybody knows, of course, that all these paintings are offered subject to stop bids, or reserves. But the reserves are secret, so you don't even know the price at which you can buy.

"It's like a tag sale, except that there's no amount on the tags.

"Now, what annoys me most is that you and I are expected to come to the auction, knowing as we do that every lot is already priced and the goal of the auctioneer is to see how much more than the owner's marked price he can get out of us. Your only chance of getting a bargain here is when the auction cataloger or the consignor makes a mistake and puts too low a reserve price on a lot.

"After the sale, if any of the buyers pay substantially more than the amount of the invisible price tags, all the dealers at the sale hightail it home to mark up the prices on their retail stock.

"I'm a collector, and I can see the price changes in some of the retail galleries the very day after a big art sale here or at Christie's."

The galleries defend their use of reserves by saying that such reserves protect owners from bidder collusion or dealer rings. They also say that unless they offer reserve or buy-in propositions to owners, they don't get consignments, and the higher the reserves they permit, the more consignments they get.

The big galleries also claim that you can easily make an educated guess at the amount of the reserve by looking at the printed estimate. The reserve, they say, is about two-thirds to three-fourths the amount of the estimate. Presumably, then, a manuscript or painting or artifact estimated at $3,000 would have a reserve of about $2,000 or $2,500. Possibly; but many times the reserves may be lower or higher.

"This damn reserve system is driving me bats," an angry collector told me. "I never know how much to bid. And I never know when I'm bidding against the gallery or when my bid limit is less than the owner's secret price tag."

"But what really galls me is all the bidding that goes on for nothing. It took me a year to figure out what was taking place. For instance, on a lot estimated at $750 the auctioneer may open the bidding at $250. Then he points here and there to invisible bidders and shouts and gets excited as the bidding mounts to $550, where it finally stops. Then the auctioneer quietly says: 'Withdrawn' or 'To order.' Of course, I'm now aware that all the bids were pulled off the pillars or the wall, just efforts to get one real live bid out of the audience. And the lot, of course, goes back to the consignor with a bill for five percent of the top legitimate bid.

"Why can't the auctioneer just open the bidding at the amount of the reserve and save us all a lot of time? This idea of 'warming up the gallery' with a lot of fake bids is for the birds."

A good point. I am hopeful that one day New York City will pass a law requiring that all reserves be printed right in the auction catalog.

Of course, a high reserve can often be a potent weapon for the gallery. There are many collectors who will bid only on very expensive items. Thus a $50,000 reserve on a $5,000 lot may result in a stunning record price for a mediocre item. On the other hand, a high reserve often acts as a deterrent to bidders who think they have no chance and therefore refrain from bidding.

Once, when I was pretty fresh at the game of the name, I consigned a one-page musical fragment of Beethoven to Sotheby's in London. I was pretty sanguinary about its chances and felt that it might bring about $750.

Sotheby's queried me: "What reserve do you want on the Beethoven? We suggest $1,000."

I advised the great auction house that I hadn't given any thought to a reserve and didn't particularly want one and wasn't aspiring to a full grand, but if it suited their ambitions they could set a stop-price in British pounds on the manuscript.

When I got the report of the sale and read that the manuscript had been knocked down to Lansberg for £320 (about $800) I was delighted. Then I learned that the manuscript had not met its reserve and would be returned to me, with a bill for cataloging it. Lansberg was but one of many code names for "no sale."

If you would like to examine the curious entry of this spurious sale in *American Book-Prices Current*, get the annual volume for 1962 and look under *Beethoven* in the manuscript section. You will find the record there, with the name of the buyer listed as Lansberg.

Fortunately most of the big auction houses have ceased the nefarious practice of reporting sales that are not sales and prices that are not prices. Such reports mislead collectors and dealers and librarians and even beguile vendors of old documents, paintings, and antiquities into a fruitless quest for imaginary buyers. I wonder if anyone with Beethoven manuscripts to sell ever tried to track down Lansberg to offer him another manuscript.

Today most of the galleries merely drop from their price lists the numbers of lots that are returned to the owners. It is a simple and satisfactory and unobtrusive way of admitting a mistake. I'm going to start doing it myself.

CHAPTER 12

Watch those Pen Scratches, Mr. President

"ONE THING A president must learn," wrote Warren G. Harding. "He never writes a letter which is read solely by the one to whom it is addressed."

Most presidents, at some time during their careers, have dropped their guards long enough to sign unusual or incriminating documents. And since everything that a president writes or has written, almost from the time he first toddles off to school, is the subject of intense interest and is a part of history, let this chapter serve as a flashing red light to the ambitious youth of the nation.

Our first president was a model of discretion in his correspondence. It is said that on the battlefield he cast off his placid mask and swore at his troops, but in his letters he never uttered so much as a "gosh" or a "darn." Among the hundreds of notes of this great man that have passed through my hands, I recall only one that even suggests impropriety. In writing to Annis Stockton, pretty wife of Richard Stockton, signer of the Declaration of Independence, Washington ventured the belief that "when once the Woman has tempted us, & we have tasted the forbidden fruit, there is no such thing as checking our appetites, whatever the consequences may be. . . ."

Washington's epistolary prudence was emulated by most of

our presidents, but now and then I run across a private letter
that gives startling or intimate opinions.

In 1975 I sold at auction an amazing letter of Dwight D.
Eisenhower's in which he castigated Robert F. Kennedy, then
campaigning for the Democratic presidential nomination.
Writing to his close friend General Robert Cutler, Ike said: "I
am disgusted at the newspaper accounts of Kennedy's recep-
tions throughout the country. It is difficult for me to see a
single qualification that the man has for the Presidency. I
think he is shallow, vain and untrustworthy—on top of
which, he is indecisive. Yet, his attraction for so many people
is extraordinary. . . ." The letter, so uncharacteristic of the
amiable Ike, fetched $3,500, a record for a typed presidential
letter.

That Ike was wary about what he signed is well known to
philographers. My close friend, Congressman Seymour
Halpern, was invited to join Eisenhower for breakfast. Since
Seymour owns a splendid collection of autographs dating back
to his boyhood, he asked me: "What shall I get Ike to sign?"

"You've got a souvenir typescript of Doenitz's order to
surrender the Nazi armies," I said. "Ask Ike to put his
signature under Doenitz's."

"He won't do it. He hates the Nazis."

"Well, give it a try, anyway. Maybe he'll sign if he's in a
good humor."

At breakfast Ike was ebullient and jovial. Seymour popped
the big question.

"I wonder if you'd mind signing something for me, Mr.
President."

"Certainly, Sy. What would you like me to sign?"

Seymour placed the typed surrender order in front of
Eisenhower who glanced at the document and saw Doenitz's
signature. His face hardened.

"Sorry, I can't sign that for you."

Abschrift.

Der Oberste Befehlshaber   Hauptquartier, den 7.5.45.
        der Wehrmacht

/Bitte in der Antwort vorstehendes
 Geschäftszeichen, das Datum und
   kurzen Inhalt anzugeben./

ICH BEVOLLMÄCHTIGE

GENERALFELDMARSCHALL   K E I T E L

ALS CHEF DES OBERKOMMANDOS DER

WEHRMACHT UND ZUGLEICH ALS OBER-

BEFEHLSHABER DES HEERES,

GENERALADMIRAL VON FRIEDEBURG

ALS OBERBEFEHLSHABER DER KRIEGSMARINE,

GENERALOBERST   S T U M P F

ALS VERTRETER DES OBERBEFEHLSHABERS

DER LUFTWAFFE

ZUR RATIFIZIERUNG DER BEDINGUNGSLKSEN KAPITULATION

DER DEUTSCHEN STREITKRAFTE GEGENUBER DEM OBERBEFEHLSHABER.

DER ALLIIERTEN EXPEDITIONSSTREITKRAFTE UND DEM SOWYET-OBER-

KOMMANDO.

DÖNITZ
GROSSADMIRAL

Nazi surrender signed by Doenitz and Eisenhower.
Sold at Hamilton Galleries, 1967, $525

"I thought, perhaps, Mr. President, since you personally were so instrumental in achieving this great result that you would not mind adding your name here at the bottom."

"I'll never sign anything touched by any of those Nazi bastards!" Ike's voice was tough and angry. He fixed a sharp, soldier's eye on Halpern.

Seymour's lower lip trembled slightly as he took back the paper. He said: "Okay, Mr. President, but you'll never know how much it would have meant to me."

Ike observed the quivering lip and relented. "Oh, hell! Give it back to me!" And he scrawled his signature under Doenitz's.

Later when Congressman Halpern overhauled and re-organized his collection he put the document up for sale at one of my auctions. It fetched $525. That was many years ago. If the same document were put on the block today it would certainly make some crashing surf in philographic circles.

Ike's letters are seldom witty. But his secretary once made a little typo (*my* for *me*) that transformed a dull note refusing to make an airplane trip into a delectable jest: "My wife doesn't like to see my fly under any circumstances." This accidental bit of humor increased tenfold the value of the letter.

Not many of our earlier presidents had the prescience to turn out the sort of inflammatory letters that regale posterity and delight historians. Or, if they did, their correspondents immediately used such letters for lighting their cigars. Zachary Taylor, a stodgy old soldier, also possessed a touch of cruelty. Taylor was so infuriated with the Indian tactics of retreating into the swamps of Florida during the Seminole War that he wrote to his brother: "The Indians have determined to use their legs instead of their arms, having climate [the tropical sun] to battle for them, which has proved much more fatal to us, more to be dreaded than their rifles and scalping knives. This unfortunate war may yet continue for many years unless the gov't employ the blood hound to aid the troops in ferreting them out."

Of the thousands of fascinating Lincoln letters and documents that have gone under the hammer at my sales, I recall only one that was slightly naughty, a masterpiece of spoonerisms. Lincoln was famed for his earthy humor and relished dirty jokes. In this little tale he captured the bawdiness of the frontier:

> He said he was riding *bass-ackwards* on a *jass-ack*, through *a patton-cotch*, on a pair of *baddle-sags*, stuffed full of *binger-gred*, when the animal *steered* at a *scrump*, and the *lirrup-steather* broke, and throwed him in the *forner* of the *kence*, and broke his *pishing-fole*. He said he would not have minded it much, but he fell right in a great *tow-curd*, in fact, he said it give him a right *sick* of *fitness*—he had the *molera corbus* pretty bad—He said, about *bray dake* he came to himself, ran home, seized up a *stick* of *wood* [sic] and split the *axe* to make a light, rushed into the house, and found the *door* sick abed, and his *wife* standing open—But thank goodness she is getting right *hat* and *farty* again—

This unsigned bit of Lincolniana was knocked down for $4,000 at one of my earliest auctions nearly twenty years ago. What would it fetch today!

If you chance upon one of Theodore Roosevelt's many letters about hunting, usually crammed with details of his kills, you might not realize that he was America's first great conservationist. Roosevelt constantly urged the protection of wild life and helped to found our continent-spanning chain of national parks. In a letter written on safari in 1909 to his friend Archie Butts, Teddy described his decimation of the

Lincoln writes a vulgar story!
Sold at Hamilton Galleries, 1963, $4,000

African jungles: "I have killed a dozen lions, half a dozen leopards and cheetahs, five rhinos, five buffalo, six giraffe, numerous boar, antelope and zebra, hyaenas, a hippo, etc. Two of the lions and one rhino and leopard charged wickedly; and I think we were in more danger from the buffalo at one moment, than from anything else. . . ." Yet this carnage was but a fly-swat compared to what Teddy did when turned loose with a high-powered rifle in the Rockies!

Wild animals were not Roosevelt's only prey. Many of his most intriguing letters took pot shots at his personal enemy, Woodrow Wilson. In February, 1915, he wrote to a friend: "Bully for you! I feel exactly as you do about Wilson and Bryan. It was infamous of them to shirk their duty about Belgium and to scream the minute the dollars were touched. It was particularly bad in view of their loud protestations that they were not concerned with dollars; were too lofty to think of them; and were only interested in humanity. Their conduct in Mexico has been atrocious beyond belief . . . the basest kind of pandering to the German vote . . . I am partly of German descent; I admire and respect Germans; but the man who comes here ought to be straight United States and nothing else. All of this is for your eye only." In another letter, written in 1916, Roosevelt was so infuriated at Wilson's adamant refusal to declare war on the Germans that he wrote: "What a dreadful creature Wilson is! I cannot believe our people have grown so yellow as to stand for him."

Teddy's cousin, Franklin D. Roosevelt, could also be rather peppery when aroused. In 1932, when he was campaigning for the presidency, there were critics who said that a cripple had no right to be in the White House. F. D. R. lashed back at "a wholly false picture. The losing of my balance and toppling is not true. I wear a leg brace to lock the knee and on one occasion, when I was speaking, the brace broke with the result that I went half way down. Frankly, I cannot see the importance of all this nonsense when I am in perfect health and get through three times as much work in the course of the average day as three ordinary men do. Come up here and watch me for twenty-four hours."

I well recall the September evening in 1965 when I sold this great letter. Only a few hours before the auction got underway at the Waldorf, a fourteen-year-old boy walked into my office with a "business proposition." A glance at his eager face told me that the auction bacillus had infected his blood stream and he was about to have an attack of bidder's fever. He was wildly eager to buy the Franklin D. Roosevelt letter. "I don't have a lot of money," he said, "but I'm willing to pledge my allowance for the next full year if I have to. I'll give you an I.O.U. if my bid is successful."

I was touched by his earnestness and, being a poor

businessman, I agreed to allow him twelve months in which
to pay, should the F. D. R. letter be knocked down to him.

Although the estimate on this remarkable letter was only
$150, I warned my youthful friend that he might have to go
to several hundred, perhaps even more. My most sanguinary
guess proved to be way off. The boy soon found himself
locked in a struggle with a Connecticut millionaire. As the
auctioneer called out the bids, one after another the other
room bidders dropped out, and at $350 only a boy and a
tycoon battled for the ownership.

"Four hundred!" shouted the boy.

The millionaire raised a pencil to indicate $425.

I could see the youngster lick his lips, and I was quite
certain he had committed his allowance far beyond the
twelve months on which we'd agreed.

"Four fifty," he shouted, waving his catalog.

Mentally, I had a picture of a youthful debtor mowing
lawns during the summer and shoveling snow during the
winter.

By now, the duel between the boy and the old man had
attracted the attention of the entire gallery. I could hear a
murmur in the audience. One man whispered: "Do you think
that boy is a shill?"

Up and up climbed the bids. Finally, as though to clinch
the matter beyond all question, the boy cried out: "Five
hundred and fifty!"

The old tycoon lifted his pencil a final time. The fight was
over.

In a way, I was happy for my young friend. I knew he'd
been crushed under a heavy load of money bags, but I also
knew that, had he won, he would have saddled himself with a
huge debt that might forever have spoiled for him the joy of
collecting and the enormous thrill of combat in the auction
room.

Many of John F. Kennedy's private letters, none of which has yet made an appearance on the auction block, abound in four-letter words and are full of Anglo-Saxon vigor and Irish wit. Some of the letters I've appraised are now salted away in archives and won't be published for the next fifty years. I envy the kids born today who may have the excitement of probing into Kennedy's intimate correspondence. I recall looking over some letters of Jack's to his first true love, about sixty or seventy handwritten notes, in one of which he rebutted his sweetheart's adamant refusal to wed him: "You are the only woman I have ever loved or ever will love." Six months later he married another woman—Jacqueline Bouvier!

A few early letters of Kennedy's have appeared on the auction market. In 1965 I sold a letter of the fifteen-year-old Jack written from the Choate School to his friend Jeffrey Roche at Lawrenceville.

I finally got out of the infirmary and the doctor said that I did not have the mumps and the nurse admitted that it was doubtful if I had the disease that you referred [to, the clap]. I heard that you had 116 girls at the dance. Choate had 135 . . .

We had Dr. Jeykily [sic] and Mr. Hyde [the movie starring Spencer Tracy and Miriam Hopkins] last night. It was pretty good and they had a good bedroom scene. . . .

The other night a member of the Student Council got me out on the track and had me running a mile and ¼ straight. He had some kind of a wire coat hanger and every time I slowed up he would smack me on the tail. He was a track man and he went as fast as hell. I was so damned pooped that I could hardly walk the next day. It was 11 at night. . . .

The letter, signed "Smuttily yours, Jack Kennedy," was

Dear Jeff:

I finally got out of the infirmary and the doctor said that I did not have the mumps and the nurse admitted that it was doubtful if I had the disease that you referred. I heard that you had 116 girls at the dance. Choate had 135 and Choate has 6 forms and none of the lower forms brought any. We won't play you in baseball till next year. We had a trackmeet yesterday and three school records were broken. The captain ran the hundred in 9⅗ but it was not counted as official because the wind was with him. We had Dr Jay K Cy and Mr. Hyde last night. It was pretty good and they had a

Boyhood letter written by John Kennedy.

good bedroom scene. School get out the eigth if you go Plan B or don't take Colledge Board and then I'm going down to Cape Cod. The other nights a member of the Student Council got me out on the track and had me running a mile + ¼ straight. He had some kind of a wire coat hanger and every time I slowed up he would so smack me of on the tail. He was a track man and he went as fast as hell. I was so dammed pooped that I could hardly wall the next day. It was at 11 at night. If you want to write Quigly write her care of American express

Smuttily yours

Jack Kennedy

write

knocked down to David L. Wolper, the Hollywood film producer, for $2,700.

In 1978 a German teacher consigned to my auction the original typescript of a speech she had prepared for President Kennedy to deliver in Berlin. The speech was phonetically written so that the president could deliver it in German, a language he did not read or speak. As this draft reveals, Kennedy jettisoned the formal speech at the last moment and delivered only the famous line, jotted on the page in his own hand: "Ich bin ein Berliner." The City of Berlin bought this great document for $8,000 and the elated purchaser said: "We were willing to go to $20,000 if necessary to get this wonderful historic treasure."

Kennedy's avenger, Jack Ruby, the man who gunned down Lee Harvey Oswald, wrote some startling letters from his cell in Dallas County Jail. That Ruby was off his rocker cannot be doubted, for in a group of notes that were smuggled to a fellow inmate Ruby accused Lyndon B. Johnson of rabid anti-Semitism and of plotting the murder of Kennedy. In an unsigned letter that I auctioned in 1966 for $400 Ruby wrote:

> Oh, who would ever dream that the——— ———
> [President Lyndon B. Johnson] was a Nazi and found me
> as the perfect set-up for a frame . . . Remember they had
> the president killed, and now with me in the picture,
> they'll make it look as though the Russians or Castro had
> it done . . . Remember the only one who had all to gain
> was Johnson himself . . . Where did Oswald get the
> information that far in advance about the future trip that
> Kennedy himself didn't know he was going to make? All
> that was planned by Johnson. No one would question the
> president about a conspiracy.

In another letter, also unsigned, that fetched $1,000, Ruby

described Lyndon Johnson's conspiracy to liquidate the Jews by freighting them secretly into concentration camps: "Stay awake these few nites and listen for the bells and the freight trains. Then perhaps after all the Jews have been liquidated . . . they [Johnson and his followers] will invade all the free democratic countries, on the pretence of being allies and then will pull the surprise of taking over . . ."

Of Richard Nixon's letters there is not much to say except that there is not much to say. In their sustained tedium his letters surpass even those of Calvin Coolidge. But Nixon's incredible signature gives some piquancy to his correspondence. It varied with his fortunes. Sometimes it is stiff and very legible, sometimes a wild, impassioned, uncontrolled scrawl in which not a single letter is decipherable. As president, Nixon signed nothing except official documents. Examples of his fourteen autopen signatures appear on letters to congressmen and senators and personal friends. When writing to Herbert Hoover, whom he addressed as "Dear Chief," he signed "Dick" with a robot. His important letters to foreign potentates bear the secretarial imitation by Rose Mary Woods. Quite a furor was roused when I pointed out in the press that Nixon's historic letters to South Vietnamese President Nguyen Van Thieu pledging American military support were signed for Nixon by his secretary.

Within a few weeks after Ronald Reagan's inauguration a spate of fascinating letters from his pen poured on the philographic market. As a movie actor Reagan had spent hours every day at his desk answering fan mail. His letters are bright reflections of his simple, honest character. When, as governor of California, he was asked to write a few verses for a literary magazine, he replied: "I agree with you. It is important that politicians show they are capable of at least trying to write poetry. It's a challenge. I'm enclosing two efforts for your consideration." Not since John Quincy

Adams published a tiny volume of "society verse" in the middle of the last century has any president or future president bent his talents to rhymes. Here's one of Reagan's poems, entitled "Time":

Budgets
Battles
Phone calls
Hassles.
Letters
Meetings
Luncheons
Speeches.
Politics and
Press Releases.
News conferences
Delegations
Plaques and
Presentations.
Travels
Briefings
Confrontations.
Crises
Routines
Meditation.
Eight years passes swiftly.
But I look out the window.
The elm in the park looks just the same.

The verses of Reagan were sold at the Waldorf-Astoria on April 30, 1981. At the same sale was a letter in which Reagan, then an "actor between pictures," wrote from London agreeing with a plan to weld the church and the lay world. "The Catholic Church has capitalized for years on those of their 'laity' who achieve some fame or success and has used them as window dressing much as a college uses a football team, etc. . . ."

In the midst of allegations that Frank Sinatra, the noted actor and singer, was affiliated with the Mafia, I offered for sale at auction a two-page handwritten epistle of Reagan in which he defended Sinatra. Writing in 1976, five years before he became president, Reagan declared:

I have known Frank Sinatra and Barbara Marx for a number of years; I'm aware of the incidents, highly publicized, quarrels with photographers, night club scrapes, etc. and admit it is a life style I neither emulate or approve.

However there is a less publicized side to Mr. Sinatra which in simple justice must be recognized. It is a side he has worked very hard to keep hidden & unpublicized. I know of no one who has done more in the field of charity than Frank Sinatra. His contributions to worthwhile causes are extremely generous but he goes beyond this. There are people on permanent pay rolls, a small town high school whose band & ball team are uniformed (he was only in the town a few days and has never had reason to go back), there is medical care for people who he has only read about in the papers.

A few years ago a small town in the midwest had suffered a terrible calamity; he went there on his own and staged a benefit to raise funds. All the expenses were paid out of his pocket, in addition to which he bought thousands of dollars worth of tickets himself and had them distributed to servicemen & police and firemen.

While I was Gov. there would come to my attention cases where there was no suitable govt. program—I would call Frank as well as others of the same nature and they

Ronald Reagan defends Frank Sinatra! Letter of Reagan held by Charles Hamilton sold for $12,500, highest price ever fetched by a note of a living person.

would organize a solution for the unfortunate people who needed help. Most of the time Frank would simply take it upon himself. Let me finish by saying that he would be very upset if he knew I'd told you these things . . .

Before the sale in January, 1981, word leaked out that Sinatra himself was going to buy the letter, no matter what the cost. The pre-sale estimate was $2,000 to $3,000. There was fierce competition for the note. After a wild epidemic of bidder's fever, gasps of amazement swept over the audience when the letter, a remarkable defense of the man so often indicted in the press, was knocked down for $12,500, exactly double the previous world's record for a letter of a living person. The purchaser was a mysterious Daniel Wolf.

And for whom did Wolf buy the letter? "Well," he told the press, "just say that I picked it up for an 'unidentified private collector.'"

CHAPTER 13

The Skull of Adolf Hitler

A T THE END OF World War II in 1945," began a letter I got from West Germany in April, 1980, "Hitler shot himself. His last wish was to be burnt. But the Russians were closing in on Berlin and there was not enough time to burn his body. In the night three of his faithful followers carried away his corpse and buried it in a private park.

"In 1953 two of the faithful dug the skull up from the secret grave, prepared it and mounted it onto a marble base. This was not known by anybody until now. The owner is in very bad financial circumstances and wishes to sell the skull, formerly the property of her late husband, a Nazi fanatic who was with Hitler when he shot himself."

This letter from Ingolstadt excited all the latent resurrectionist in me. I've always been intrigued by skulls, the *memento mori* "death reminders" of the Middle Ages and often the symbol of secret societies whose members toasted one another from a cranial goblet. The poet, Lord Byron, drank his claret from a skull. Hamlet delivered the world's greatest soliloquy while contemplating Yorick's skull. Throngs in the shires of old England still ooh and ah as they look at the skull of Cromwell, a treasured relic, whenever it's placed on exhibit. The skull of Charles XII, king of Sweden, is on display in Stockholm and reveals the gaping hole near his right eye where a sniper's fatal bullet struck him in 1718. In the ancient cathedrals of Europe the mouldering skulls of the saints still perform miracles. And I once sold for five dollars the freshly dug up skull of James Peale, the noted artist, and then plunked down the fiver at a nearby bar to toast "the memory and genius of old Jim Peale."

So why shouldn't I auction off the skull of the world's greatest mass murderer? I'd spent four tough years in the army during World War II hoping to bring home this very trophy. And now here it was, offered to me.

I wrote to the owner and requested more information. His reply added only a few new "facts" but a great deal of misguided emotion.

Mr. Hitler shot himself and Eva Braun on April 30, 1945, in the building of the Reichskanzlei in the city of Berlin. My friend, Herr Adolf Wagner, and two other gentlemen brought the two corpses out of the building in order to burn them as Mr. Hitler had ordered. While they were doing this the Russians arrived in Berlin and the fire was put out. At that time of war everything was upside down in the city and the Russians did not know and also did not care whose corpses they were. Frau Wagner's husband and one of the men managed to escape, the third was captured by the Russians. His name was Heinz Linge. After the Russians left, the two other men came back and buried the scorched bodies in the park of a nearby villa. In 1953 the relics were dug up by the two men. They did not do this in order to sell the bodies or make any profit. No, they wanted to give these Nazis a resting place of honor. The head of Hitler was prepared and mounted onto a marble base. Hitler was a god for them, a holiness they believed in.

At my request the owner crated the skull and mailed it to me. He and I were aware that if any custom's official got wind

The bullet hole in "Hitler's skull." Charles Hamilton points to entry point of bullet. Notice on the skull the superbly preserved front teeth—the incisors and canines.

that Hitler, or any part of him, was crossing the Atlantic and coming into the United States, there would be an international incident. The owner cleverly attached to the box containing the morbid relic a declaration of contents: "1 ea. Skull for spiritual sessions."

Within a month I found myself opening a large cardboard carton wrapped in plain brown paper. A brief examination of the skull, sardonically grinning on a base of black marble, convinced me it was not Hitler's. I set the remains down as those of a suicide or murder victim.

The teeth did not resemble those in an X-ray of Hitler's skull taken after the bombing attempt on his life in July,

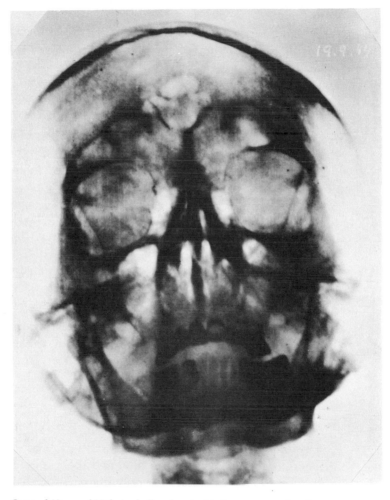

Original X-ray of Hitler's skull, taken by his doctors soon after the
attempt on his life, July 20, 1944. Observe the extensive fillings and bridgework
(dark portions) on his teeth.

1944. The X-rayed skull revealed teeth with extensive fillings and bridgework, all lacking in the skull that had just arrived from Germany. I had sold the original X-ray several years earlier and was, of course, familiar with Hitler's mouth, a dental disaster. In the second place, the holes in the skull indicated that the trajectory of the bullet, from the point of entry to the heavily fragmented point of exit, was slightly downward and would require that a right-handed suicide hold his pistol at an awkward angle.

I at once telephoned my close friend, Dr. Michael Baden, the New York Medical Examiner and formerly in charge of the committee that had exhumed and autopsied the remains of the late President John F. Kennedy.

In less than an hour, Dr. Baden was in my office examining the skull with great interest and curiosity. His preliminary conclusion was the same as mine: It wasn't Hitler's skull. Dr. Baden suggested that since the dental work was of paramount importance in identification, we also get the opinion of Dr. Lowell M. Levine, New York City's expert in forensic dentistry. Early in July, 1980, Dr. Baden and Dr. Levine, together with Dr. Clyde C. Snow, a forensic anthropologist, gathered in my gallery to examine the skull and deliver a final opinion in the presence of Richard Severo, a reporter from *The New York Times.* Severo described the results of the conference:

Hitler is said to have committed suicide by swallowing a cyanide capsule and shooting himself in the head. There is a bullet hole in the skull and there is evidence that the skull was opened for an autopsy.

Mr. Hamilton estimated that if it really was Hitler's skull, it would be worth at least $100,000 to a collector. Asked why anyone would want it, he replied: "Hitler is the supreme criminal of all times. He out-Neros Nero, he out-Caligulas Caligula. Therefore, he is a most fascinating man."

The three experts examined the skull and agreed not only that it was not Hitler but that it was not even what the Nazis called "Aryan." The experts said the skull appeared that of an Oriental. Two of them noted that it had certain characteristics that made it look almost female, such as a flattening of the brow area. They finally agreed, however, that it was the skull of a man.

The scientific analysis of the skull illustrates how dentistry, anthropology and pathology have joined forces in contemporary medical examiners' offices in major cities . . .

For the analysis of the "Hitler skull," Dr. Levine, a forensic consultant to both the New York City and Nassau County medical examiners, armed himself with dental records compiled over a 10 year period by Dr. Hugo Johannes Blaschke, a brigadier general in the Waffen SS, who was Hitler's dentist from 1934 until 1945.

Dr. Blaschke left behind notes and sketches of the inside of Hitler's mouth indicating that the dictator had a severe periodontal disease and a great many cavities, as did many other high-ranking Nazis. "They were very fond of pastries and whipped cream," explained Dr. Levine. Hitler also had gold bridgework, made by Dr. Blaschke . . .

In contrast, the skull sent to Mr. Hamilton had very good teeth and no bridgework. Moreover, the front incisors were shovel-shaped, suggesting that the skull was Mongoloid, not Caucasoid. "There is no way these teeth can be Hitler's," Dr. Levine said.

Dr. Snow . . . who has been asked to identify many plane crash victims, noted that the lower portion of the jaw of the skull was "not typically Caucasoid" and that the person may have been Oriental or of an Oriental-Negro mix.

Dr. Baden noted that the bullet hole was in the temple, whereas Hitler was said to have shot himself in the mouth. Dr. Baden went over the Soviet autopsy reports, however, and said he was surprised to learn that the Russians had missed the gunshot wound and attributed death only to the cyanide. After Hitler died, an aide was said to have tried to burn the body beyond recognition with gasoline, and the skull was badly charred, which would have made the bullet hole more difficult to find.

Dr. Baden could find no evidence of charring on the bogus Hitler skull. He suspects that the skull, which contains some evidence of plaster of paris, was once used as an anatomical specimen for students.

It's always possible, of course, that Hitler's faithful followers, Heinz Lange and Adolf Wagner, carried off the corpse of a stand-in for Hitler, a man whose body was accorded a Viking burial while the real Fuehrer made good his escape from the Bunker.

Or, on a more frivolous note, the discrepancies can easily be explained: The charred skull that the Russians dug up was that of Hitler late in life, with all his dentures and fillings, whereas the skull mailed to me is that of the more youthful Adolf, with his teeth still in excellent condition.

CHAPTER 14

Letters They Should Have Burned

I F YOU'VE EVER wanted to be a peeping Tom or a prying Pamela but never had the nerve, then you'll enjoy this chapter because I'm going to let you read some of the private letters that have passed through my hands during my two decades as an auctioneer. Now and then, I must confess, I've been threatened with legal action for putting intimate notes on the market, but thus far I've eluded the talons of the law.

Most famous people are wary about stripping their souls naked on paper. Whenever they write about confidential matters they tab their letters: *Burn this* or *Not for publication*. Such injunctions merely inspire the recipients to bundle up the proscribed notes in pink ribbons and docket them for a nosy posterity.

Hollywood has turned out its spate of sizzling epistles and steaming diaries. I once sold Errol Flynn's own penciled record of his early adventures in New Guinea, sexual and otherwise. Flynn had abandoned the notebook after he took sanctuary in a nunnery and then fled, leaving a lot of unpaid bills. The sisters who consigned this strange document explained that there were many raunchy passages that they had expunged with scissors. What remained of this chronicle of Flynn's youth was a plate glass view into his mind. For a proposed essay on "the art of seduction," Flynn noted some topics: "Compromising (without trousers) positions to avoid—avenues of escape must be arranged first. Avoid

betraying astonishment at credulity of victim, even in the
dark. Draw analogy between the mention of the word
'marriage' & he who uses dynamite in exasperation after
having failed with dry fly—use of alcohol to be deprecated
except as a last resort." In another vein he wrote of his little
room: "Coloured prints of Christ are regarding me dolefully.
He is portrayed in a large variety of postures. Why is it that
Christ is never shown smiling? Thank God I brought 2 bottles
of Rum and the Bible, and will thus have both drink and
something to read."

Flynn outlined his philosophy of life, a credo that he later
carried out: "I am [going] to see if I can learn what life has to
teach and above all *not* to discover, when I come to die, that
I have not lived. I am going to acknowledge not one of the
so-called social forces which hold our lives in thrall & reduce
us to economic dependency. The best part of life is spent in
earning money in order to enjoy a questionable liberty during
the least valuable part of it. To hell with money! I am going
to live Spartan like. I refuse to accept the ideology of a
business world which believes that man at hard labour is the
noblest work of God. . . ."

This remarkable thirty-seven–page diary fetched only $160
in 1970, an era when microcephalic collectors and historians,
of whom I was one, had not yet realized the immense cultural
importance of motion pictures and the artists who created
and performed in them. Ten years later, on January 17, 1980,
a mere two-page letter of Flynn's rocketed to $650. Burned
out with booze, drugs, and sex scandals, Flynn wrote from
Spain on July 12, 1957: "I sold my Gauguin painting some
months ago to pay off debts—fair price $110,000 cash. My
Van Gogh—you recall?—I still have. If your client is
interested I would sell same for $140,000 net to me.

"I have no home in the U.S.A. and no present intention
of having one, having become subject to violent attacks of

nausea at the mere thought of living in California. I would be willing to part with the Van Gogh. What the hell's the use of a beautiful work when you have no place to hang it? It's like living with a woman without sexual *écroutement* [a French vulgarism] profitless."

The revulsion felt by Flynn at Hollywood was shared by others. Tyrone Power, waiting to start work on *Ladies in Love* with Loretta Young, wrote from Beverly Hills to a close friend in New York: "I've heard how hot it's been in N.Y. and it really must be something. Even at that I'd take it in preference to this hell trap any time." In a letter to Anita Loos, Aldous Huxley bitterly complained that Claude Rains had walked away from a picture because he wanted more money and the studio manager had said: "Not even Jesus Christ could get a raise in salary." Huxley added: "It would make a splendid subject for a religious painting—the Savior before Mannix, Katz and Mayer [studio big shots] pleading for a hike in his wages. . . ." Montgomery Clift wrote to a close friend in 1941: "We saw movies being shot in Hollywood, which is a horrible place." Hollywood later revenged itself by destroying Clift, who took little solace in his friendship with other actors. In another note dated 1946 (knocked down for $500 in 1979) Clift wrote about an accidental encounter with Van Johnson: "This guy is conceited & self-indulgent to a degree you wouldn't believe. And he only has one topic of conversation: Van Johnson. Any effort on his part to talk about anything else is so painful to him that you feel sadistic if perhaps you talk about the weather. The changes of subject revolve around phases of his career rather than whole new topics."

In a letter to author Lawrence Quirk, the great silent film star Mae Murray unburdened a tortured soul about her quarrels with Louis B. Mayer in Hollywood: "My trouble started in the 30s and no one came forward to help me. Most everyone bowed to this evil man [L.B. Mayer] and feared he would harm them if they did not bow to him. In 1926 my life was rich and happy, the world knows this, so you would be wrong to print anything contrary to the truth. . . ."

Many remarkable letters of Rudolph Valentino have passed through my hands. There was a bundle of youthful correspondence penned at fifteen to a close friend in which the future film star enclosed the visiting card that had got him into trouble when he passed it out to chorus girls: "I picked up the clap from one of these ladies. From now on I'm going out only with nice girls." In February, 1980, I sold at the Waldorf-Astoria for $800 the most pugnacious letter ever written by the great Italian-American idol. It was addressed to a journalist who had attacked Valentino's masculinity in *The Chicago Tribune:*

> You slur my Italian ancestry; you cast ridicule upon my Italian name; you cast doubt upon my manhood. This is not a challenge to a duel in the generally accepted sense. That would be illegal. But in Illinois boxing is legal, so is wrestling. I therefore defy you to meet me in the boxing or wrestling arena to prove which of us is more a man. I hold no grievance against the Chicago Tribune altho' it seems a mistake to let a cowardly writer use its valuable columns . . . I will have an opportunity to demonstrate to you that the wrist under a slave bracelet may snap a real fist into your sagging jaw.

You might not suspect that Ed Sullivan—placid, smiling, hunched-over—was really a feisty, tough Irishman in disguise, but a confidential letter to a friend revealed Ed in fighting trim. Describing a public dispute with Walter Winchell, Sullivan got hot under the collar all over again as

he talked about his brawl with the weaselly columnist in the
old Reuben's restaurant:

> It was the night I had done my first Broadway column
> [about 1931] on the Old Graphic, and I deliberately put
> in the zing for Winchell-type columnists who "in their
> search for realism, lift covers on garbage cans."
>
> I sat down at your uncle's [James Quirk's] table. While
> Winchell glowered at me, I got into a breezy discussion
> on various things with two friends. Winchell, unable to
> stand the silent treatment any longer, finally exploded:
> "Were you referring to me in your column today?" I
> assured him that I hadn't referred to him and he yelled in
> a loud voice, so that the whole restaurant could hear
> him, "Well, so long as you have apologized to me it is all
> right."
>
> At this point, I leaned across the table, grabbed him
> by his necktie and yanked him across the table toward
> me, so that he looked like John the Baptist being
> beheaded. In an equally loud voice, I told him: "As a
> matter of fact, you slimy bastard, I did mean you, and if
> you say one more word—even if you say yes or no—I'll
> take you downstairs to the men's room and fracture you."
>
> With that, I flung him violently back into his chair—
> made my apologies to your uncle for disturbing the peace
> at his table, and left the restaurant.

Among the duels with attorneys that I've embarked on was
the one over an extraordinary letter of Ingrid Bergman to
"Dear Kay" about Bergman's notorious affair with Italian film
director Roberto Rossellini. The letter was penned in 1949
and exactly thirty years later I put it on the auction block.
The defiance of marital bonds by Bergman and Rossellini had

caused an international shock wave. The lovers had a child
before Rossellini could get an annulment or Bergman a
divorce. The affair resulted in Bergman's exile from Hollywood for many years. Writing at the height of the scandal,
Ingrid eloquently defended her character and poured out her
heart to her friend, Kay. Bergman blamed R.K.O. studios for
capitalizing on her romance with Rossellini. About her lover,
she wrote: "I cannot remember anyone in Hollywood taking
such ridicule, such lies, such a beating in the press. I waited
for R.K.O. to stop these stories. But in opposite they added
more." Bergman described how R.K.O. sent a "spy" to watch
her, "but he was as poor a spy as he was a publicity man." Of
her husband Peter Lindstrom, Bergman wrote: "I realize
Petter was not himself and suffered like a beast in this
scandal. . . . Petter sends letter after letter with insults and
abuse about Roberto. What good does it do to talk against or
forbid love?"

Movie stars and their associates like to sue people. A good
law suit is as essential to an actor as a good suit of clothes. No
sooner was this letter published in the papers than I got a
peremptory demand from Kay's lawyer. Either I remove this
anguished note from my auction or Kay (Katharine Brown)
would file a court order to bar its sale. I dutifully took the
letter out of the sale and, a few months later, on behalf of the
consignor, sold it privately to a collector in California.

In the summer of 1980 I had a skirmish with Liza
Minnelli's attorney over some Judy Garland papers and
photographs that had been found some twenty years ago in a
house that Judy had hastily moved out of. The papers were
offered to Judy who refused them. With a group of fan letters
and other tributes was Liza's French notebook, kept when she
was fourteen. "I am still madly in love with Bobby Darin,"
she confessed in an unfinished letter to her mother tucked in
the notebook. Also in the notebook was a letter to Judy

The glamorous eyes of Liza Minnelli. Drawing in her French notebook by Liza when a young girl.

Garland from her third husband, Sid Luft, promising: "Somehow all your unhappiness will go away. You deserve better than this and it will be." But to me the most delectable part of the notebook was a pair of seductive eyes, doubtless Liza's own orbs sketched by the future star in 1960.

I turned the collection over to the consignor who, after some pusilanimous negotiations, sold everything to Liza Minnelli for $1,000, $200 of which he paid me to soothe my ruffles and defray my costs.

Among the great scientists of the world Albert Einstein must take rank as a brilliant letter writer. His notes are crisp, powerful, intimate. To fellow professors in Germany who sought to emigrate to America he frequently issued the warning that professors are abundant and not highly esteemed in this country and "the devil shits on the highest pile." In a letter dated after the entry of the United States into World War II, Einstein apologized for an earlier statement that "the man who enjoys marching in line and file to the strains of music falls below my contempt; he received his great brain by mistake—the spinal cord would have been amply sufficient." The atoning letter was written in October, 1944, to Private Albert Sherwin of the United States Army: "I have changed my attitude. . . . Against organized violence nothing can help but organized power. Without it all peace-loving people would be enslaved or even annihilated."

A record price of $5,000 was paid at my auction on April 10, 1980, for a pathetic letter of Einstein's (1916) describing his anguish over the divorce from his first wife, Miza:

> The separation from Miza was, for me, a matter of survival. Our life together had become impossible, even depressing. So I am giving up my boys, whom I love tenderly . . . I find that my children do not understand my ways and harbor a sort of anger towards me . . . though painful, it is better for their father not to see them any more. I shall be satisfied if they become effective and esteemed men.
>
> I shall never approach Miza again. I will finish my days without her. I dedicate all my thoughts to reflection. I resemble a presbyopic person who is charmed by vast horizons and who is disturbed only when an opaque object prevents him from seeing. . . .

Einstein's great contemporary, Sigmund Freud, wrote equally dramatic but more clinical letters. He and Einstein never really understood or appreciated one another, although both were agnostics. In a note to my close friend, the late Reverend Cornelius Greenway, Freud wrote: "I think I may not claim a place for my portrait in a church when my attitude towards religion is so unrelentingly negative." This letter was sold with other effects of Greenway at Sotheby Parke Bernet in October, 1970, and fetched $425.

PROF. SIGM. FREUD

Jan 75th 1939

20 MARESFIELD GARDENS,
LONDON, N.W.3.
TEL: HAMPSTEAD 2002.

Dear Sir

I have perused your letter with great sympathy, but I think I may not claim a place for my portrait in a church, when my attitude towards religion is so unrelentingly negative.

By the way I possess no photographs of mine, all of them having been destroyed in the Nazi invasion. The one taken here is so unsatisfactory that I want it not to be in circulation.

Yours respectfully,

Sigm. Freud

Sigmund Freud refuses to permit his portrait in a church.
Sold by Sotheby Parke Bernet, 1970, $425

As a rule great generals are not great letter writers. Napoleon and Custer, both colorful war heroes, were exceptions. In a letter of Napoleon's that departed my podium in exchange for $2,300 the emperor demoted the pope to the post of glorified lackey. "For the pope's purposes, I am Charlemagne. My empire, like Charlemagne's, marches to the East. I therefore expect the pope to accommodate his conduct to my requirements. If he behaves well, I shall make no outward changes. If not, I shall reduce him to the status of Bishop of Rome."

Love in the kitchen was the subject of one of Custer's flammable epistles to his first love, Mollie J. Holland of Cadiz, Ohio. In a letter signed "Bachelor Boy," the future Indian fighter, only seventeen years old and a school teacher, revealed himself to be a skilled con artist. "That occurrence at the kitchen the other night . . . I cannot help but think very strange of you in relation to that affair . . . I am the last one to countenance what might be called forwardness in young people. I would look upon a young lady who would act towards every young gent as you did with me or as I got you to do very reluctantly. I cannot see wherein we were acting wrong in doing what we did that evening considering the relation that exists between us . . . how much freedom ought there to be between you and I. I am afraid that even if we were married (which I hope will be in time to come) you would place improper bounds upon our treatment of each other and be too much in favor of formality like some old ancient Lord and Lady of England."

Authors make the best letter writers and many times their most casual and disarming epistles pass quietly and forever into the realm of literature. This is not because authors express themselves artfully but because they possess a unique honesty, an ability to utter exactly what is on their mind without dissimulation. Notice how direct John Cowper Powys is when he discusses his creative processes in a letter to actress Asta Fleming Sullivan: "I steal from great poets their ideas—give them the devil knows what twists of my own & proceed to claim them as mine! But I can't help it. I am a born Thief of Literature, a Pick-Pocket of literary ideas—an Egoist patched together with papyri stolen from ancient shrines. . . ."

Brief and pungent are the notes of H. L. Mencken, the prickly sage of Baltimore. In a letter to Alexander Kadison he wrote: "The American people hate good English, and soon or late they'll get rid of it. I begin to believe seriously that within another century *I seen* and *I done* will be taught in the schools." Mencken might be interested to learn that although these grammatical crimes are not yet encouraged in the universities, there is another sort of bastard English being taught, for I hear it constantly from the college students! George Sylvester Viereck, the noted poet and journalist, complained to George Bernard Shaw that his son Peter Viereck, soon to win a Pulitzer prize for poetry, had jettisoned the traditional language of bards. Replied the ninety-one-year-old Shaw: "Peter must be a precious greenhorn to be taken in by all that guff about XIXth century English being obsolete and unintelligible, and replaced in the classics by the slang of Hollywood bartenders."

Before we leave the master of brevity, H. L. Mencken, and enter the province of the apostles of the four-letter word, I'd like to pave the way with a few pithy words from the Baltimore sage: "I am against any sort of censorship. It is always stupid and usually it is also dishonest. I think the laws should be amended to throw responsibility on complainants. As things stand, any virgin monsignor or Y.M.C.A. snooper is free to drag an innocent author or manager into court. No play ever written was ever half so filthy as the mind of the average volunteer censor."

The school of scatalogical scribblers, comprising virtually all of the greatest writers of the last half century, also turned out the most readable letters. D. H. Lawrence's notes, many of which I have sold at record prices, are noble and dignified. In a letter that I sold for $250 in 1965—it would command at least $1,000 today—Lawrence wrote to Mabel Dodge: "Don't think of the world any more. Leave that to me. I am more cunning, and being alone, one must be a serpent as far as the world is concerned. As for the fight—subtly and eternally I fight, till something breaks in me. . . ." In 1927 Lawrence discussed in a letter his new novel, *Lady Chatterley's Lover*, a book destined to be pounded by the critics and censors and banned in America. "The novel is so 'shocking' from the smut-hunting point of view that no publisher would dare have the ms. in his office," wrote Lawrence. "From my point of view, it is an assertion of sound truth and healthy reaction against all this decay and sneaking perversity which fills most of the books today. I consider my novel pure in the best sense—and warm-hearted. But the Puritan will want to smite me down." This prophetic letter fetched $700 a decade ago but would easily bring five or ten times as much today.

The most prolific correspondent of this century was Henry Miller. He acquired pen pals from his mail box and to all of them he wrote bundles of letters, all filled with complaints about his poverty and lousy health. In 1955 he bitched to Robert Fink, to whom he wrote nearly 250 letters: "Unless I receive help soon from those I call my friends I am sunk. It seems impossible for me to borrow anything like the sum I need. In my extremity, the only solution I can think of is to ask if you would be willing to send me a dollar a week, or a dollar a month until the crisis is over. Wrote Huxley and T. S. Eliot recently, asking for a loan of a thousand. No luck. Both ill and Huxley strapped. Eliot can't send money out of England." In another letter Miller recriminated against his rotten luck: "When shit becomes as important as money, the poor will be born without assholes."

The maestro of oblique communication and fractured spelling, Ezra Pound, was a prolific correspondent. He manufactured a new style out of four-letter words and used them as nouns, verbs, adjectives, and any other part of speech that he could wedge into his verbal assaults on society and literature. His letters always fetch high prices at auction. Pound expressed his opinion of censorship in a letter written from Vienna in 1928 that was knocked down at my August, 1980, sale for a resounding $1,600: "I consider the law under which *Ulysses* [by Joyce] was suppressed an outrage, the people who tolerate such a law little better than apes." You will not often discover a "proper" sentence like that one in the morass of Pound's letters, nearly all of them freighted with weird neologisms and scatalogical forays. In a letter penned in 1931 Pound posed for meditation the subject "whether a nation that fails to provide me with 50 bucks a month ought to consider itself a nation or a shithouse."

William Carlos Williams, known as "Water Closet" to his friends in college because of his initials, combined explicit language with clear prose and crystal thinking. His letters command premium prices on the block, but he wrote so many that they are usually offered in bundles. In a letter dated 1953, he commented on Jack Kerouac, whose philosophy he sympathized with but whose name he couldn't spell: "Kaouak [sic] was out here with a bunch of his Zen-budist [sic] pals last summer, 5 of them. They were dressed as bums, they were bums, they hung around most of the afternoon until Louis Ginsberg, father of Allen Ginsberg, called for them. Karouek [sic] had a black eye from jumping out of a rear apartment window to get away from an irate husband . . . Writes standing on his head or in any other position to get the thing down while its hot, a man that will do anything . . . told the

world about him to ———— itself and took to railroading
before he became a bum—but never a loafer."

On a melancholy note, Williams advises a friend: "Keep
your pecker up, god knows mine has passed out years ago but
then I am a poet long used to that sort of thing." He tells his
correspondent, Fred Miller, his theories of life and art in a
letter dated 1943: "There ain't no other way to take a virgin
but by violence no matter how disguised. The lions in front of
the Library in the city roar every time a virgin passes.
Violence is one of the phases of creation, gentleness is the
other. A mind that is incapable of violence is likely to poop
itself out . . . The martyrs for resignation and abnegation are
men who are more intolerant than any violent fucking whore
and ripper ever was. They want to rule me and you and
everybody else by subterfuge and legal scheming. They are
fakes. Catholic and Protestant alike they keep mum when
their very earthy interests are concerned. Did the Pope come
out for the spirit in Spain? Like hell he did, he came out for
the Church. The spirit has few champions or none at all in
the world. Were there one, they'd cut his balls out the
moment they'd catch him."

The most exciting letter writer of our century, in my
opinion, is Ernest Hemingway. I predict that long after his
other writings are dust-piled, a thousand or so years hence,
Papa's letters will share a noble shelf with the epistles of Pliny
and Cicero, Keats and Byron, Mark Twain and Shaw. Not
everybody, of course, had even heard of Hemingway while he
was alive. In a letter written from Havana in 1939 to his sons,
Patrick and Gregory, Hemingway commented on the ano-
nymity he enjoyed with his servant man:

> Reeves continues to be wonderful. The other night he
> says to me, "Mister Ernest what for you never tell me
> youre an important man? Why you hide that from
> Reeves?"

I asked him where he got that idea and he said he met a man in the Cuban telephone company and he ast him who was his boss now. Reeves says Mister Hemingway my boss now. Mister Ernest Hemingway? the man say. You mean who writes all those books? Yes sir, Reeves said Mister Ernest Hemingway as fine a gentleman as ever drew breath or I mixed a drink for but I done know nothing about no books. Yes sir, the man say. He writes books. Fine books and I read every one he ever wrote and my wife she read some too and she say "They good. They really good."

What for you never tell Reeves you write books?

Well, Reeves, I said, I've asked you a hundred times not to bother me nor let anybody in because I was working on a book.

Oh, said Reeves, I didn't know you meant that kind of books. I thought you work on books like book-keeper books. I didn't know. You just sit in there all by yourself with just pants on and no shirt and write those reading books. . . .

What I would like to be is A Fugitive from a Typewriter. . . .

Hemingway was often accused of impotency and even cowardice. In a magnificent letter to John A. Parker, Papa spelled out his feelings toward women and writing: "I may write about women very badly, but I love them very much . . . Have never slept alone, when I could help it, except when I was fighting. I have fucked every woman that I ever wished to fuck and many that I did not wish to . . .

"Never had some soul shattering experience with some woman nor suffered a hidden wound. Have had the clap from women but never held it against them. Have been wounded by men, armed, 16 times and know the dates, the places and the nature of the wound."

Hemingway describes how two surgeons had wished to remove a blood clot from his head by operating. "I argued them out of it on the grounds that my head was my writing machine. If they fucked up my writing machine I might end up as a door-man at the Hotel Vendome. Have the necessary military ribbons and am tall enough to be a door-man almost god-damn anywhere. But would rather write. A writer writes about half the time when he is pissed-off. I always write feeling good or pissed-off. When you are pissed-off the critics call it The Tragic Sense of Life . . ."

This letter was knocked down in 1960, after fierce bidding, for $1,100. Today it would fetch many times that sum, for the four-letter language that was taboo two decades ago is now the parlance of the parlor.

Hemingway himself tagged this great letter for posterity by writing on the envelope: *Personal: For Mr. Parker only.*

CHAPTER 15

Murder's the Game of the Name

EVERY NIGHT, just before she climbs into bed, Rosina Belpedio tenderly kisses the picture of a man she loves but never met, the murderer, David Berkowitz.

Rosina shares a tiny hotel room in Brooklyn with her black-and-white cat, Mendelssohn, but she has invited Berkowitz ("Son of Sam") to move in with her if and when he gets out of prison. Like millions of others, Rosina is fascinated by evil and is so enthralled by the 44-caliber killer that she wrote him an admiring and sympathetic letter.

Berkowitz wrote back: "There are a lot of things that can never be, such as, the two of us getting together. Wherever I am going, it will be for a long time, too long. I don't think we could ever get together, it just cannot happen."

Shortly after the forty-year-old Rosina got this reply from Son of Sam she turned it over to me for sale, but with some trepidation. "I wouldn't want to arouse his ire," she said, "if you know what I mean." The letter fetched $400 in my auction of September, 1977.

I've often been criticized, sometimes with scorn or vehemence, for selling letters by Berkowitz, Charles Manson, Albert De Salvo ("the Boston Strangler"), and even Lee Harvey Oswald. Oddly, my critics, many of them auctioneers and dealers, have no compunction themselves about peddling letters of Professor John W. Webster, who cudgeled and then dismembered his Harvard colleague, George W. Parkman, in 1849, or Lizzie Borden, who chopped (or didn't chop) up her

155

parents with an ax in 1892, or John Wilkes Booth who in 1865 blew a gaping hole in Lincoln's head. It appears that blood is less red and murder less heinous after a few years pass.

The sale of Berkowitz' letter to Rosina triggered an influx from other pen pals of the notorious killer. His letters to Dee Channel, his "mother confessor," are redolent with saccharine remorse. Often in the same letter Berkowitz' handwriting and spelling degenerate abruptly and a new personality, maudlin and vicious, takes over. In a series of penciled notes to Dee he wrote:

> I'm a Christian now, you know. I give my life to Jesus and I promise to serve him. This, however, does not mean that I'm free of the demons because I can still feel their presence often . . .
> There is no such thing as demon possession. It is, as far as I'm concerned, all nonsense. Take your nonsense and leave us alone . . .
> I know that I am no cold blooded killer and I don't hate girls. I want to be forgiven of my sins and be with Jesus when I die . . .
> I doubt if we would ever see each other in heaven because if I do get to heaven Jesus will only cast me out into outer darkness . . . if I really was a Christian, then I am the worst, lowest and foulest child of God ever. I'm no child of God. Rather, I am a child of Satan. How can you call a vile soul like me a Christian? I am a modern day Judas. It would be better for me to have never been born . . .

In December, 1978, I got a letter from an inmate, David Knatz, at Marcy State Prison where Berkowitz had just undergone psychiatric tests prior to his transfer to Attica.

Letter from Abe Lincoln's assassin fetches record price at auction

The Associated Press
BOSTON

A letter written by President Abraham Lincoln's assassin two months before the 1865 slaying sold at auction Sunday for a record $68,000 US.

In the letter dated Feb. 9, 1865, John Wilkes Booth asks a friend to send him a picture of himself "with cane & black cravat" — the one later used in his Wanted poster.

The previous high for a Booth letter was $38,000 US, according to Stuart Whitehurst, vice-president of Skinner Inc. auctioneers.

The buyer was Joe Maddalena, a Beverly Hills, Calif., historical document dealer. Maddalena said Booth "is the rarest American autograph."

"When he killed Lincoln, anybody who had any relationship with him burned their letters, because they were so afraid they would be linked to him," Maddalena said. "There are only 300 known letters and he must have written thousands and thousands."

Whitehurst estimated that only 17 Booth letters remain in private hands. This letter was addressed to family friend Orlando Tompkins of Boston, an apothecary and part owner of Boston Theatre. Booth tells Tompkins he "will get any letter sent to Fords Theatre."

Booth was retrieving his mail at the theatre on April 14, 1865, when he heard that Lincoln would be attending *Our American Cousin* that evening. Booth, a Confederate sympathizer and former actor, returned during the play to assassinate the president.

Also auctioned was memorabilia from President John F. Kennedy's personal doctor, Janet Graham Travell, the first woman to serve as White House physician. The autographed copy he gave her of his book, *Profiles in Courage*, sold for $5,500 US.

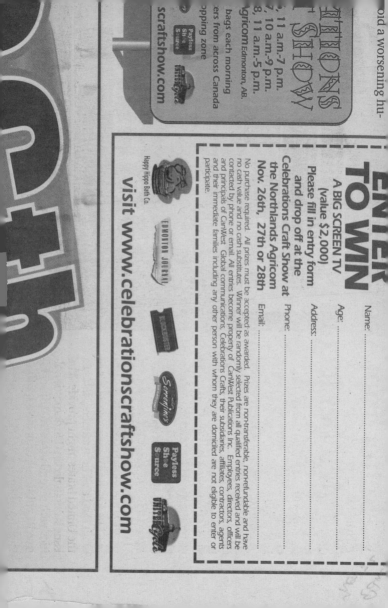

Knatz wrote: "I am trying to sell autographs, notes of Son of Sam. Do you think you could help me?"

Knatz, I later learned, had a record of 34 arrests and was in stir for manslaughter. He had struck up a prison friendship with Berkowitz who, in a rare moment of intimacy, explained to Knatz the real reason he gunned down couples in parked cars. It wasn't that he was urged on by demons. "Berkowitz is

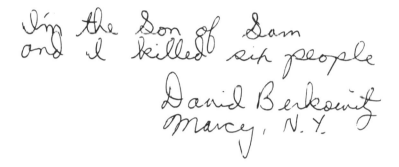

Confession of Son of Sam! David Berkowitz signs an unofficial admission that he killed six people. Sold by Hamilton Galleries, 1979, $350

an adopted baby and thats how his mother became prignent. Having sex in a car. Sam wanted to put a stop to all this (onwented babys being born)."

Knatz mailed me several little "confessions" penned by Berkowitz: "I am the Son of Sam and I killed six people." And: "To whom it may concern. If you didn't get me by Wenesday I would have killed 100 by Saturday." I sold these two macabre documents for $625. Knatz, meanwhile, had transferred to Attica where he renewed and strengthened his friendship with Berkowitz and was prepared to get more "confessions" from Berkowitz.

Ever since the first letter of Berkowitz to Rosina had passed
through my hands, I'd publicly maintained that Berkowitz
could not possibly have written the famed Son of Sam letters
that were widely publicized in the newspapers. On radio and
on television I many times stated that Berkowitz had an
accomplice and that the cops should reopen the case. Now,
with my pipeline to Berkowitz through Knatz, I felt certain I
could prove my contention. I told Knatz to ask Berkowitz to
make a drawing of the demons that possessed him (which I
regarded as nonexistent) and to write a note signed with his
Son-of-Sam signature, a weird symbol embodying the shield
and spear of Mars and the mirror of Venus.

At this point Berkowitz' conservator got a court order
demanding that I cease and desist from selling Berkowitz'
prison autographs and that I refrain from further correspondence with David Knatz. At my attorney's insistence, I signed
a compliance with the conservator's demand that forever
closed the iron door on my access into the aberrant mind of
this notorious killer.

Recently, however, since the death of Sam Carr (whose
dog supposedly inspired Berkowitz), the cops have belatedly
probed into the possibility that Carr's son, John Carr, a
recent suicide or murder victim in Minot, N.D., may have
shot some of the victims and written the neat, artistically
styled Son-of-Sam letters sent to the police by the 44-caliber
killer.

There's a revolting postscript to my sale of Berkowitz'
letters. A youthful collector recently showed up in my gallery
with a big package under his arm.

"I've got something here you'll like," he said, as he
unwrapped a huge framed ensemble.

Then he held up a colored photograph of Berkowitz,
matted and surrounded by the portraits of his six victims.
Ornately displayed beneath Berkowitz' face was his penned

and signed confession: "I am the Son of Sam and I killed six people."

"That's the most disgusting object I ever set eyes on," I said.

"You mean you won't sell it at auction?"

"You're demented," I said angrily. "Get that damnable thing out of my gallery before I lose my temper and smash it."

What this young man failed to understand is that Berkowitz, although a symbol of unreasoning evil and a major figure in the history of American crime, should not have his murders commemorated. To frame his portrait is to enshrine the act of brutal and senseless killing.

Another murderer whose letters are most revealing is Charles Manson. His penciled notes, crudely scrawled and often filled with oblique sallies into the realm of mysticism, are darkly mysterious and as impenetrable as the mind that created them. Manson is a William Blake with a bloody dagger in his hand: "And I don't spell your english as well as a jerking jaw, or cat's paw reaching from darkness to play with your queen's toung," he wrote to a friend in England. "I'm held down in ways of others playing realitys, of dreamers dreaming dreams or dreams dreaming dreamers. . . ."

Jettisoning punctuation and grammar and spelling as he flogs a wild Pegasus, Manson continued: "I play with out madness in dull sleep with walking dead & minds mouthing meannlyness [meaningless] words from men long in graves of King james & Engling [England's] mother sent her children to my cross & prays to death of a million marters in who's name praze a fool for only a fool could keep the center of his mind under the spinning world less a hole be put in his head by Sain men looking for them selves in side my own eyes are hot & hide from my voice because its vibrations is concitered out burst. . . ."

In the summer of 1978 an enormous man entered my

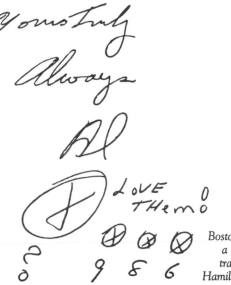

*The weird signature of "the
Boston Strangler." Conclusion of
a letter of Albert de Salvo to a
transvestite "pen pal." Sold by
Hamilton Galleries, 1979, $100*

gallery and introduced himself as the owner of a small, itinerant carnival. "I've had some pretty unsavory associates at times," he said, "and one of them conned me into buying this little collection of letters."

From his coat packet my visitor extracted a tiny bundle of seven typed letters, all signed by Albert De Salvo, the Boston Strangler. "The only reason I'm willing to part with these," said the big man, "is because I've got a chance to buy a new and thrilling 'ride' for my carnival. The price for the ride is only $80,000 and I've got to raise a couple of thou to clinch the deal."

As I studied the letters a feeling of revulsion assailed me. The hackles on the back of my neck rose and stiffened with every fresh wave of disgust. Writing from prison, De Salvo had poured out his sexual fantasies to Roy, a young man he'd never met, in pornographic language that would have shocked the Marquis de Sade. Never had I so completely peered into the mind of a brutal murderer.

After a brief negotiation I bought the letters. When I read them more carefully I realized they provided a unique insight into the most vicious criminal of modern times. Mash notes to a transvestite lover, "Roy," they included a photo of Roy in drag, posing, at De Salvo's suggestion, as Roy's sister, "Rose," so as not to arouse the suspicions of prison censors. All the letters were written in 1972, only a year before the Boston Strangler was stabbed to death by a fellow prisoner.

To adventure into the mind of this despicable monster who subjected his women victims to torture and rape before killing them is a terrifying experience. Someday, I have no doubt, an enterprising psychiatrist will collect the letters of sex-motivated murderers and through a careful study of them will uncover fresh insight into their aberrant minds—and, who knows, he may find better ways to cure them.

CHAPTER 16

The "Dear Ros" Letters

A VERY NERVOUS lawyer was Theodore Donson! His eyes blinked, his lips trembled, and his fingers fluttered as he produced from his briefcase six dainty missives in the beautiful, cursive script of Jacqueline Kennedy Onassis.

"My client would like to offer four of these for sale in your next auction," explained Donson. He produced a visiting card that identified him as an attorney. "If possible," he went on, "my client would like an advance of $500 against the future proceeds."

I noticed that the letters were penned to "Dear Ros," who seemed to be a very close friend of Mrs. Onassis'. They certainly merited the requested payment. Donson kept back two of the six letters, as well as the original envelopes. "My client would prefer not to have his name known," said Donson.

"Very likely these letters will get a lot of publicity," I said. This apparently gratuitous remark was inspired by Donson's nervousness and was designed to put him into a precipitous retreat if he'd stolen the letters. All thieves abhor publicity.

"Splendid," said Donson. If he felt any trepidation there was no hint of it in his pale face.

Donson signed the contract prepared by my secretary and I handed him a check for $500.

Neither he nor I had the slightest inkling that in three days the letters would be printed on the front page of every newspaper in the world. Or that their publication would cause a serious rift, one that would never heal, between Jackie and her tycoon husband, Aristotle Onassis.

It seems that every time I handle a letter of Jackie Onassis' it's a traumatic experience. I think that's because she's such a flamboyant and exciting personality that anyone who has anything to do with her finds himself caught up in a net of intrigue and mystery. There is vastly more interest in women with picturesque pasts than there is in women who are virtuous churchgoers.

I was much excited about the letters to "Dear Ros" because they were very intimate. They weren't exactly love letters, but, like all Jackie's delicate epistles, they were whimsical and witty. I could understand why the recipient of the letters wished to remain anonymous and had instructed Donson to hold back the envelopes of the letters.

No sooner had the lawyer walked out of the door than I made one of the biggest mistakes of my career, a career that's included thousands of foolish, little errors and hundreds of egregious blunders. I decided to send photocopies of the letters to Maxine Cheshire, a columnist for *The Washington Post*, whose gossipy articles were widely syndicated. Maxine had confided to me a few days earlier in a telephone conversation: "Charles, you and I are good friends. Do keep me in mind for anything new or unusual, especially about Jackie O." Maxine had a sweet, beguiling voice with a touch of magnolia in it.

The letters to "Dear Ros" or "Dearest Ros" did not strike me as anything more than friendly missives. The earliest was penned on White House stationery on April 18, 1963, and the last, on stationery bearing the name of the yacht *Christina*, was written during her honeymoon cruise with Aristotle Onassis and datelined from Greece on November 13, 1968. The final letter indicated that Ros, like most of

Jackie's friends, had little inkling of her intention to marry Onassis. From Greece Jackie wrote:

> Dearest Ros—I would have told you before I left—but then everything happened so much more quickly than I'd planned.
> I saw somewhere what you had said and I was very touched—dear Ros—I hope you know all you were and are and will ever be to me—With my love, Jackie.

The reference to "what you said" was an allusion to a statement made by her correspondent, who I later learned was a member of Kennedy's cabinet, when informed that Jackie had eloped to Greece. "I hope," he had said, "that she has a happiness that certainly is entitled her. I wish her that."

Two of the earlier letters are really only short notes. The first, written from Palm Beach in April, 1963, reads:

> Dear Ros—It was so thoughtful of you to write me about the baby—It is such a happy thing and thank you so much for taking the time—And now that I don't have to go to all those ladies' lunches I hope I can come and see you and Madelin some lunch in May or June— Sincerely, Jackie.

In January, 1965, she wrote:

> Dear Ros—It was so thoughtful of you to send John that helicopter—You can imagine how he loved it—You wrote me a letter that I think about a lot—I am grateful for what you said—I know you understand. With love, Jackie.

The longest letter, and the one that will interest historians

the most, was written while Jackie was still first lady and was
dated June 13, 1963:

Dear Ros—I did love that insidious slim little volume
you sent me—it is just the sort of thing I steep myself in
all day long and will be writing poor imitations of when I
am an old lady—

Did you send complimentary copies to your colleagues
in the Cabinet? I was wondering if Dean Rusk or
Anthony Celebrezze would be interested in establishing
such a relationship with me—now that the Deputy
Secretary of Defense is leaving—

I feel that the Defense Department is much too rugged
terrain for those little seeds to take root—Though
General LeMay might be the most rewarding of all—And
I could hold up cue cards of what he was meant to say
next—

Why are you so cruel to send me such a book—When
the only not too chic a restaurant I can repair to with my
friend is the Navy mess.

I loved my day in Maryland so much—It made me
happy for one whole week—It is only Thursday today—
But I know the spell will carry over until tomorrow—And
I will go back to Camp David—And see those West
Virginia motel shacks with their bomb shelters churning
underneath—as great white columned houses—

We had some people to dinner last night who had been
to another farewell party for you at Anderson house. I
always push unpleasant things out of my head on the
theory that if you don't think about them they won't
happen—

But I guess your departure—which I would never really
let myself realize until tonight—is true—

I feel sorry for whomever succeeds you—(For them)—

And I will never really like them—No matter who they turn out to be—And neither will anyone else—They will always live in your shadow—And no one else will be able to have force and kindness at the same time—

But I feel much sorrier for us—in this strange city where everyone comes and goes so quickly you get rather used to its fickle transiency—So when anyone's departure leaves a real void—You should be really proud of that— Although you are the last person who would care about such a thing.

I know you will find some peace at last—But I also know that the change of pace will be an awful readjustment. I wish you so well through all of that—

Please know Dear Ros that I will wish you well always—thank you—Jackie.

When these letters reached Maxine Cheshire's desk she phoned me at once with a ring of fiendish glee in her voice: "Oh, Charles! These are *wonderful* letters. Exactly what I was looking for. Everyone here in Washington knew that Jackie and Roswell Gilpatric were dating and these letters prove it."

Maxine added some lurid details about Jackie's life as first lady. I had the feeling now that Maxine was on the scent and would run her quarry into the ground. I was already sorry I'd sent her photocopies.

Half an hour after Maxine's call came a telephoned appeal from Gilpatric, former Deputy Secretary of Defense under Kennedy. "These letters were stolen from my locked safe," said Gilpatric. "Who brought them to you?"

I broke my rule not to identify consignors in view of the accusation of theft leveled against Donson.

"Donson worked for me and when he left he took these letters with him," said Gilpatric. "Can you get them back from Mrs. Cheshire? If they're published they'll end my friendship with Mrs. Onassis. She'll never speak to me again."

Gilpatric reminded me that he and I had met several times. His voice was tremulous, with a tone of desperate urgency.

"Are you sure you didn't authorize Donson to sell these letters for you?" I asked.

"Absolutely not!"

"Okay, let me see what I can do," I said.

"I'm a member of *The Washington Post* board of directors," added Gilpatric, "but they tell me they never meddle in Maxine Cheshire's business. I've put all the pressure on her that I can. Please help me."

I was determined to get the photocopies back and to kill the story.

Maxine accepted my call, but the magnolia in her voice was now tinctured with rat-bane. At first I urged, then I pleaded and finally I begged. "There's no need to hurt Gilpatric," I said. "It won't serve any purpose." But the Cheshire Cat was not smiling. Her claws were sharpened and she would not move. The best I could get from her was an amorphous assurance that she'd "consider" my request not to print the letters.

About six o'clock the next morning Gilpatric telephoned me and the quaver in his voice suggested that he was crying. "The letters are on the front page of *The Newark Star-Ledger*," he said.

"Damn! That means they're all over the world."

Gilpatric asked me to return the original letters to him. I agreed, but I wanted to make certain that he had had no hand in their proffered sale. "I'd like to make this a police matter," I said. "And I want to make sure the thief is prosecuted." Although Gilpatric was opposed to calling the district attorney's office, he finally agreed.

Two detectives picked up the letters and that ended the

case of the purloined letters except for a string of aftereffects.

While the storm over the letters raged and thundered through the newspapers and editorial writers screamed about yellow journalism, Art Buchwald made merry over the whole affair. In his column on February 21, 1970, he joshed:

> A few days after the publicity of Mrs. Onassis' letters a man walked into my office and said he had four letters he would like to sell me, written by Ros Gilpatric . . .

Buchwald complained about the high price asked so his visitor offered him some other hot merchandise, all of which Buchwald spurned. Finally the mysterious vendor made his best offers:

> "All right, then," he said, opening his valise. "For $200 I will sell you 10 letters from the New York State Democratic Party, asking for contributions to draft Arthur Goldberg for Governor of New York. Before you protest, I would like to remind you that you would own the letters of a party to whom the man to whom the woman to whom the man to whom Mrs. Kennedy Onassis once wrote 'With my love, Jackie.'"
>
> "Do you have anything cheaper?"
>
> "Here are some letters from Arthur Goldberg for $100. These letters, all authenticated, were sent out by Mr. Goldberg, denying he had any ambitions to run for Governor."
>
> "But they're so far removed from the Jackie Kennedy Onassis letters."
>
> "How can you say that?" he said. "They were written by the man who was supported by the party which was appealed to by the man who received a birthday greeting from the man who was the owner of the original letters

written by Jackie Kennedy Onassis from the Yacht
Christina the day after her marriage to Onassis. What the
heck do you want for a hundred dollars?"

The publication of the very private "Dear Ros" letters had
provoked some bitter editorial attacks on Maxine Cheshire
and *The Washington Post* and, of course, the usual arrows of
malevolence directed at me. But the distinguished columnist,
Max Lerner, described the whole situation with aplomb and
sanity:

> Sensational yellow journalism? I don't think so.
> Prurient reader prying into what is nobody's business? No,
> not that either. Partly a natural human feeling for the
> human. Partly the recognition that a public person
> doesn't stop having a private life, except that the private
> life becomes more difficult, vulnerable and more distorted
> when some of it spills over into public scrutiny.
> Consider how it is: An attractive woman writes a half-
> dozen warm and romantic letters to a man she has come
> to know well since he worked with her husband. He
> treasures them enough to lock them in his office safe,
> from which they are somehow extracted and put up for
> sale. An uproar follows, not because the letters are
> extraordinary—other women have written much the same
> letters—but because the woman's husband was President
> before he was killed, and she herself was once an
> American queen and has never stopped having an ex-
> regal appeal—that of an abdicated, if not a deposed,
> queen. . . .
> Of course the most sensible way of dealing with the
> current episode would be to dismiss it with a shrug, and
> turn to some other things that count more. But I suspect
> that many men would secretly have liked to be the man

who received those letters, and many women would
hanker to be the woman who sent them. That may be
where the episode belongs—not in the history of
changing American manners and morals, but in that of
the fantasy life of Americans.

Despite the jocularity of Buchwald and the wisdom of
Lerner a lot of people got badly hurt by the publication of the
"Dear Ros" letters:

—The least harmful effect was that my relations with
Maxine Cheshire chilled and I took the first chance to sever
totally and forever my association with her.

—For days after the story broke, Aristotle Onassis, then in
New York, walked slowly past my midtown gallery every
afternoon and paused to glare ominously into the big windows
that opened on the street. Maybe he wanted to pitch a bomb
into my gallery. He was certainly justified.

—Gilpatric's wife filed for divorce the day after the letters
were published.

—Onassis changed his will and cut Jackie out of everything
except $20 million and a share in his yacht.

—And Theodore Donson, who started it all, refunded my
money but later got picked up on charges of stealing rare
prints from a library. He was tried by a jury of his peers and
quietly vanished from the public eye.

CHAPTER 17

Nazi Relics up for Grabs

THERE WAS A DAMP, charnel smell in Hitler's bombed-out Bunker," the ex-sergeant told me. "The floor was flooded and the fetid water was over my ankles. I'd bribed a couple of Russian guards with cigarettes and here I was, scrounging for Nazi souvenirs among huge piles of smashed furniture, wet papers and rubble. Finally I spotted a large filing cabinet that appeared to be untouched, a possible source of choice loot.

"As I put my hand out to open the top drawer of the cabinet I got the scare of my life. From a shoulder-high shelf just above the drawer an evil, living face was peering at me, a face with a stubby moustache and sharp nose and piercing eyes. For one awful moment I thought it was Hitler himself. Then I realized it was an enormous rat, probably rendered fearless by hunger. I drove him off by waving my arms. In the file under him, I discovered this volume."

A huge swastika gleamed on the cover of the massive book the ex-sergeant placed in my hands. The dreaded Nazi insignia was formed of very dark amber set in a field of light yellow amber and rimmed with flashing silver. There was a horrifying beauty to this jewel-like volume from Hitler's library. It was a gift to the Fuehrer from Danzig, giving him the freedom of the city. Within the covers was an ornate parchment scroll signed by all the local dignitaries.

When I subsequently sold this historic book at auction it fetched only $500, but that was long before the Nazi "craze."

Today it would bring several thousand, at least. Many such "city freedoms," beautifully bound and heaping encomiums or laudatory verses on the Fuehrer have passed through my hands. Sometimes they are inscribed on great rolls of vellum, aflame with color. They typify the flamboyance and arrogance of the Nazi regime, an era of ornately crafted daggers and bayonets, gold-braided uniforms that suggest ritzy doormen, certificates and diplomas in rich Gothic script, and medals wrought with cunning designs in bronze and silver.

In the past twenty years I've sold at auction thousands of Nazi relics and documents. And nearly always such sales have evoked criticism, harrowing experiences, or even threats on my life.

Once I placed in the window of my old shop at Madison and 53rd Street a signed photograph of Hitler that was featured in a forthcoming auction. It was elegantly encased in a special silver frame that bore Hitler's initials and the Nazi insignia. Less than an hour after I put it in the window my secretary handed me a note that had been quietly pushed under our front door: "Get that signed photo of Hitler out of your window, or we will throw a bomb in your gallery." The note was unsigned.

"An idle threat," I said, since my desk was not close to the window.

"Maybe," said my secretary, "but a well-placed bomb would land right on me. Either Adolf goes or I go."

It was an easy choice. Adolf went.

Today the big threat to me is not from bombs but from collectors who are stampeding me and other autograph dealers in their frenzy to stock up on letters and documents of Hitler and his henchmen before the price goes through the roof. A letter of Hitler's is now worth five of Churchill's and ten of Franklin D. Roosevelt's.

Who's in the Third Reich rat race? The Germans are

Unpublished self-portrait of Adolf Hitler. Drawn by the future dictator when an army dispatch rider, about 1915. Notice the inept draftsmanship. The club-like hand is nearly as big as his head. The feet gave the artist so much trouble that he simply left them out. And the famed "hypnotic eyes" of Hitler couldn't transfix a clam!

buying. The British are buying. But most of all it's Jewish collectors in America. They bid with aliases or anagrams, from behind pillars or half-closed doors, or signal the auctioneer furtively. Their names are top secret.

Is it just the fascination of evil and violence? Maybe. But as one Jewish collector explained to me: "It's like having the head of the hunter on the wall instead of the hunted."

One of the outstanding Nazi collections in America was formed by the late Philip D. Sang, whose collection of Judaica I recently appraised for presentation to Brandeis University. I helped Sang to build his superb assemblage of Jewish letters and documents and I helped him to gather his huge and very important Nazi collection. Among the historic items that came from my sales were the Nazi top-secret plan for the invasion of Holland and Belgium and Mussolini's own copy of Nietzsche's *Man and Superman,* annotated with Il Duce's own ideas for implementing the philosopher's vision.

Another Nazi collector, famed for his physical education courses, once told me that his entire family was wiped out in an Austrian concentration camp during the Holocaust. Yet I never met any man so enthralled by the Nazis, especially the more brutal of them. He liked to ensconce his villains in spectacular frames. I once put together for him an "ensemble" of Hitler and Goering, with examples of some of the medals worn by the Fuehrer and his pompous air marshal. As my customer stood admiring the finished product, glittering with medals, he commented on my "superb job" and I couldn't refrain from asking: "What are you going to do with it?"

"Why," he said, "I'm going to hang it in my living room."

I couldn't think of any reply except: "Not the place I'd pick to hang Hitler and Goering."

Whenever I put Nazi autographs and relics up for auction there is always an instant reaction from the press and the public.

Guy Martin of *The Soho Weekly News* came to one of my sales that included some Nazi relics. His description of the affair is so devastatingly accurate that I'd like to quote a few paragraphs from it:

> The question of the hour is, what kind of people buy stuff like this? Lean, skull-faced men standing in black leather overcoats and riding boots in the back of the room raising their crops in the air: "von million Amerikan dollrs . . . two . . . zree, zree million for zee ahm-band . . ."
>
> As it happens, the Charles Hamilton Gallery (25 E. 77th St.) is a major dealer in autographs of historical figures and other memorabilia, and none of its customers, or at least very few of them, seem to be neo-Nazis . . . And, in the interests of proportion: of the 379 lots sold at the auction last Thursday only 11 had anything to do with the Nazis . . .
>
> Everything about the main room of the [Conrad's] suite, every aspect and accessory, means *money*. The gold ceiling is well over 20 feet tall, and the walls are lined with broad, gilt-framed mirrors which stretch all the way up to the molding. In the center of the left wall is a chest-high red marble fireplace. Over the floor-length windows on the right side of the room hang abundant, orange-and-gold curtains, gently parted.
>
> The buyers are seated in two sections of about 75 people each. The upholstery of their chairs is a fine gold brocade . . . There is a predominance of middle-aged males in dark suits . . . The crowd is peppered with young couples . . . The auctioneer welcomes us in a nasal baritone and briskly opens the bidding. In the aisle, cameramen hook into their battery packs and begin to film him . . .

The Channel 2 TV people turn their lights and cameras back on the audience and begin to move up the aisle to the back of the room . . . I stand up and follow them out into the smaller room in the back where yet another camera crew has Charles Hamilton himself at a small table in the corner. Spread out in front of Hamilton and his interviewer are most of the Nazi mementos: a few dark-looking medals, the armband [of Hitler], a pile of post cards and pieces of paper.

Hamilton is a slight, dapper man with a shock of white hair falling across one side of his forehead, a la Carl Sandburg. He wears a dark suit. He is very quick in his movement and accommodating but emphatic in his speech, a manner which constrasts strongly with the oily attitudes of the newsmen around him . . .

"Why do people buy these things?" asks the newsman.

"People collect such things as these because, basically, evil is the most fascinating thing in the world."

The newsman had not anticipated this sort of direct response and fishes for a moment for his next question. Although Hamilton is clearly the right man to speak with, it is apparent that the newsman is not getting the story that he wants. He asks Hamilton for an opinion of Adolf Hitler, and Hamilton tells him that Hitler was the most evil man in the century . . .

The armband, that choice little piece, eventually sells for $1100 to an unidentified buyer. The World War I Iron Cross goes for $575. Another pays $200 for the wound medal, while the Nazi Party membership pin nets $325 . . . the auctioneer moves to the sixth Nazi lot, a pair of embroidered towels from Hitler's Munich house. They sell for $190. In the next lot, No. 305, is yet another embroidered towel, which is, as the catalog describes it: "slightly stained, else fine." It is some time

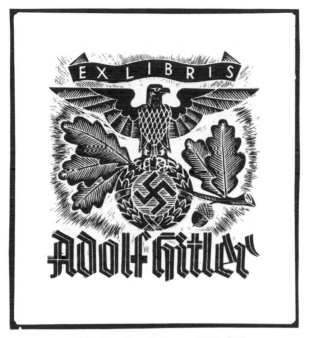

Hitler's bookplate. Sold by Hamilton Galleries, 1979, $75

before I realized that what is actually being auctioned off here is the man's dirty laundry. Truly—here is a story for all those newsmen who failed to find the filth they were so earnestly pursuing . . .

Things loosen up a little in the back room. A camera crew, elbows firmly planted on the small bar in the rear of the room, is drinking cold Heinekens. Appropriately enough, Hamilton is giving his autograph to two kids from a junior high in Brooklyn. I ask him how he felt it went.

"Oh, I think it went extremely well," he chuckles, eyes a-glitter. "I think even Adolf Hitler would have been pleased."

I tell him it is the first auction I have attended.

"How do you like it?" he asks. He seems genuinely interested. "The most amazing things happen, you know. Junky things go for a lot of money, and good things go for very little."

We part for a while. Later I see him sitting at the table in the rear of the auction . . . His feet are curled around the legs of his chair like a schoolboy's.

Quite often I've sold relics of ordinary Nazi soldiers. Enough Nazi flags to equip an "army terrible with banners." Medals sufficient to decorate the chests of a whole regiment. Bayonets and daggers by the score, all of them ornately wrought in gleaming steel and bronze. And, on rare occasions, Nazi caps and jackets, remembrances of long ago when my constant daydream was to catch Adolf Hitler in the sights of my carbine.

On March 23, 1978, I offered at auction, among other relics of World War II, an original large-size dress uniform tunic bearing the full shoulder and sleeve rank insignia of a Nazi sergeant-major of artillery, 71st Regiment, accompanied by a dress hat ornamented with a spread-eagle holding a swastika. As I am not personally acquainted with any neo-Nazis and most collectors of Nazi relics eschew uniforms, I wondered who would buy these unpleasant mementoes.

The afternoon before the sale I was visited by an enormous Prussian with an enormous moustache and an enormous voice.

"I am Heinrich von Papen-Manstein," he boomed at me in a thick German accent.

When I was unimpressed he puffed his body up like a blowfish and added menacingly: "Remember zot name!"

From a briefcase he extracted several letters written in ink on large sheets of expensive paper and illustrated in pencil with drawings of soldiers. They were signed *Adolf Hitler* but bore little similarity to other letters of the future dictator written during World War I.

"What are these?" I asked.

"Letters of Hitler, orichinal letters, written durink Vorld Var Vun."

Usually when I spot a forgery I try to let the owner down gently, but von Papen-Manstein's overbearing and patronizing manner irritated me and I decided his fat, Goering-like derrière could withstand a good thump.

"These are fakes," I said, "blatant fakes. The ink is 'wrong.' And where do you suppose Corporal Hitler would get such elegant paper? Furthermore, these letters were never even folded to go through the mails."

"Hitler zent dem flat."

"From the front? Quite impossible. And look at the

Ziegler zu unterrichten.

Hitler's signature shrinks! TOP: *Hitler's signature in 1939, from a directive sold at Hamilton Galleries, 1979, $550*
BOTTOM: *Hitler's signature from a directive about bolstering the Russian front, initialed by Keitel, sold at Hamilton Galleries, 1979, $3,600. Observe that after six years of war, facing utter defeat, the arrogance has gone out of Hitler's signature, and it is only half as large as it was at the peak of his power. Hitler shot himself several months later, on April 30, 1945.*

handwriting. Not even a good imitation of Hitler's."

My visitor appeared unconvinced. No doubt he had put hundreds, perhaps thousands, of dollars into these elaborate forgeries. As I got ready to leave my gallery for another appointment, he launched into an angry monolog on my ignorance. No sooner had I closed the door behind me than he turned to my secretary and curled his lip in scorn:

"So zat ees Charles Hamilton!"

The next evening von Papen-Manstein attended my auction at the Waldorf-Astoria and bought the jacket and cap for $120.

I presume he found them an excellent fit.

In November, 1975, I put up at auction several unusual Nazi items, one of which instantly captivated the press. It was an ornate, gold-plated license plate used on Hitler's parade limousine. He'd presented it to his mistress, Eva Braun, because she was intrigued by its flashing beauty. The plate was made of heavy brass plated in gleaming gold. There was an embossed swastika in the upper left and a Nazi eagle in the upper right. The plate bore the legend: "Reichskanzler—Deutschland."

Not more than two doors away from the Conrad Suite at the Waldorf-Astoria where I was holding the sale of Hitler's license plate, there was by chance a meeting of the B'nai Brith, an assemblage of pensive graybeards wearing yarmulkes. A television reporter perceived the anomaly.

"May I borrow that license plate for a few minutes?" he asked.

"Of course," I said.

I followed him and his television crew into the B'nai Brith conference. The reporter selected an old man who looked as though he might have suffered the brutalities of a concentration camp.

"Sir," he said, "Mr. Hamilton, the autograph dealer, is

auctioning off, just down the hall, this license plate from Hitler's limousine. May I have your opinion on the sale?"

"Disgusting! I cannot believe that anyone would sell or buy such a revolting object."

The reporter asked the same question of three or four other elderly members of the assemblage. The answers were all vehement denunciations of me and my auction.

After the license plate was sold for $3,500 to a Jewish dealer, the reporter asked me what I thought of the sale.

"A lot of people may wonder why such a relic can command such a high price," I said. "It's simply explained.

"It is a part of the history of the world, albeit an unpleasant part. But no amount of sentiment or wishful thinking is going to change history.

"If we don't preserve these gruesome reminders of the past, we may forget and allow the same thing to happen again."

Here are a few random prices fetched by Nazi relics at my auctions:

A photograph signed by the pig-faced Ernst Roehm, head of the brownshirts, $1,250

Signed photograph of Adolf Hitler, large size, $1,100

Typed document, weirdly signed in crayon by Hitler during the final days in the bunker, $6,500

Soup ladle from the Fuehrer's dinner service, $625

An important letter signed by Field Marshal Erwin Rommel, $2,000

First edition of *Mein Kampf,* one of 500 signed copies, bound in creamy vellum, with a lengthy inscription to a close friend, $10,000

Handwritten letter by Adolf Eichmann, implementer of the Holocaust, denying his guilt, $1,000

Blotter from Hitler's desk, $100

Award of the Knight's Cross of the Iron Cross, signed by
  Hitler, $2,500

Original envelope that contained Hitler's will, certified by
  Dr. Lammers, Chief of the Chancellery, $3,000

Important early letter of Hermann Goering's, $400

Original engagement book of Heinrich Himmler, chief of
  the Gestapo, $5,000

Collection of 12 ornate pieces of Hitler's stationery, $750

I've sold large numbers of unused sheets of stationery and
correspondence cards of Hitler's. They always attract eager
buyers. Like other American soldiers in Europe near the end
of the war, I often used the stationery of Hitler or other
leading Nazis to write home. I frequently couched my letters
in comic German, most of my vocabulary consisting of
ludicrous adaptations of English into German. Once my mail
was censored by a stupid lieutenant of the semiliterate variety
that abounds in every army. He accused me of being a spy.
For weeks afterward he was the butt of ridicule from every
officer and enlisted man in our outfit.

In the fall of 1979 a young man, who introduced himself as
Aaron Goldberg, brought me for auction a small sheaf of
unused stationery imprinted with Hitler's name and address.

"I take it your father brought these back from Germany
after the war," I said, recognizing the paper as that often used
by Hitler in writing to lower army echelons.

"No," he explained. "My father was too old for the army.
He owned a printing shop in Brooklyn. Two or three years
before we got into the war, he was asked by the Nazi embassy
in New York to print some official stationery for Hitler. It was

tough at that time to get any sort of work and although
Jewish, my father took the job. I found these sheets in the
back of his shop."

Contrary to popular belief, Hitler was never a house
painter but was, in fact, an artist who actually made a meager
living from his watercolors of flowers and buildings and street
scenes. Several years ago I had a visit from my good friend,
Shea Tennenbaum, a distinguished Hebrew poet, and our
conversation fell upon art and artists.

"A great artist paints from his soul, not from his mind,"
said Shea. "It is this flood of deep, inner emotion that makes
a great artist."

"Don't you think that an artist can counterfeit emotion?" I
asked. And without waiting for a reply, I walked to a file in
my gallery and took out a small watercolor of flowers in a
vase. "What do you think of this?"

Shea studied it. "Obviously," he said, "the artist was a man
of great delicacy and profound feelings, a lover of beauty. He
has captured the supreme moment in the existence of these
flowers and recorded it with taste and skill."

I said: "Look at the signature in the lower left."

Shea looked and gasped in horror. The signature was that
of Adolf Hitler.

For a moment I feared that Shea might slump to the floor,
but he very quickly recovered himself and I apologized for my
prank.

After Hitler had twice failed the matriculation test for the
Vienna Academy of Arts and Sciences—he had hoped to
become an architect—he turned to dabbling in watercolors.
His favorite subjects were deserted streets, public buildings,
and churches. A friend of Hitler's, Reinhold Hanisch,
pretended to be blind so he wouldn't need a peddler's license
and hawked Hitler's paintings for him in the bars of Vienna.
They sold for a few kronen each and the two youths split the

Hitler the artist. Painting in watercolors by Hitler, done in Munich, about 1913. Hitler's signature is at lower left. Sold at Hamilton Galleries. Hitler's paintings fetch between $5,000 and $10,000.

take, much of which they spent on pastries and whipped cream. At this time Hitler was bearded and wore a derby and a long black coat that gave him a very Semitic appearance. Oddly, most of his regular customers were Jewish, and since Hitler was fond of quoting Jewish proverbs he was often taken for a Jew.

In 1913, to escape the Austrian draft, Hitler moved to Munich where he continued to dash off mediocre paintings of churches and cathedrals. The future dictator was turned on by cold stone. He had a love affair with mortar and granite. When he tried to paint people, their faces were distorted and their limbs looked like clubs or pedestals.

Hitler's paintings, in dark grays and greens, often seem to be stage settings for some awful Senecan drama. Yet there are many collectors who seek to own one or more of these somber creations. Those who compete furiously at my sales for Hitler's aquarelles are not art collectors or neo-Nazis. They are World War II buffs, most of them ex-soldiers who fought against the Nazis in the great war.

Hitler's paintings were often counterfeited, even while he was alive. There are three or four fakes for every genuine painting on the market. The authentic ones sell for around $5,000 to $12,000, depending upon their quality.

The bottom line on Hitler the artist? When Heinrich Hoffmann, Hitler's personal photographer, asked the Fuehrer to permit an exhibit of his work, the dictator scowled and said: "Absolutely not. My watercolors do not belong on the same walls as our great German painters. After all, Herr Hoffmann, I was a pretty lousy artist."

CHAPTER 18

The Thief with
the Patriotic Stationery

I'M A BULL'S-EYE for thieves. As their favorite target, I sometimes sit in my office and muse over who'll be next to hit me with a heisted Washington or a hot Lincoln. Even as I write these lines there's no doubt a crook somewhere figuring out how to knock me off. At this very moment, I venture to say, a deft-fingered fellow in some great library has just slipped into his pocket a rare document with which he'll test my alertness and detective skill. So far I've been lucky. I've nailed fifteen crooks, forgers, or thieves, and put them all behind bars.

This story is about one of the most daring and dextrous of them, a clever young man who eluded me long enough to disrupt my auction sales and create mayhem in academic circles.

As a twenty-five-year-old college student, Ronald Ellis Wade began his career by losing a close primary for state representative in his home town of Gilmer, Texas. The loss was not without benefits. Wade emerged from the contest with a sheaf of red, white, and blue stationery that bore the legend "Ronald Wade/State Representative" in enormous letters on a star-bedecked banner. He put this imposing letterhead to work at once by conning three Dallas photographers who had witnessed the murder of Kennedy in 1963 into supplying him with photos and accounts of the tragedy "for

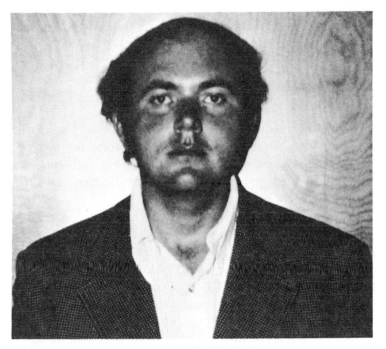

Photo of Ronald Ellis Wade

the state museum's memorial to Kennedy." There was no museum and no memorial except in Wade's larcenous mind.

Once Wade discovered the value of his illicit stationery he turned it to an even more profitable account. I was his first mark. On January 31, 1975, he wrote me:

> At the request of the Texas Presidential Museums I have been asked to help dispose of several duplicate items in our collection to help finance new purchases.
> I enclose two interesting items, an October 5, 1960, two-page letter from Harry Truman urging party support of JFK-LBJ, and an October 20, 1960, letter from John Kennedy re brother Ted.

If you are interested in purchasing one of these or both you may send your bid by a check—return if you are not interested. We reserve the right to refuse your bid subsequent to comparison with another bid we have received.

It might strike you as odd that "the Texas Presidential Museums" was de-acquisitioning unique letters, but museums move in mysterious ways. Wade's stuffy letter and impressive stationery fooled me. I was completely taken in, and Wade quickly wriggled his hand into my wallet.

Among the treasures mailed to me by the defeated candidate and victorious thief were half a dozen letters by Lyndon B. Johnson. Since the "Presidential Museums" was in a hurry for coin of the realm I bought the letters outright and then plopped them into my auction catalogs.

Meanwhile, it later developed, Wade had kept his deft fingers busy looting the University of Texas and the Texas State Archives in Austin. He crammed a huge suitcase with what his mother later called "political trivia." Now and then Wade parted with one of the gems in his new collection, but for the most part he hoarded his treasure. The suitcase got fatter and fatter and traveled everywhere with Wade. When things eventually got overheated in Texas the youthful heister journeyed West to California and set up new head-quarters at La Quinta near Los Angeles.

"Wade's plan," I later told a friend, "was to strip the libraries at the University of California at Los Angeles and the University of Southern California of their most salable documents, then lam out to fresh pastures. So long as he kept moving and suckers like me kept buying he could add to his personal collection and make a modest living without risking capture."

Posing as an ardent research worker, the youth with the

patriotic stationery conned U. C. L. A. officials into letting
him pour over their archives. Every visit he paid them added
to his already superb collection of precious documents. After
several months of plundering Wade got ready to split. To
raise cash for the move he decided to make a final killing,
with me as his victim. He clipped the library of my alma
mater, U. C. L. A., for a big bundle of historic boodle,
including a rare document by Lincoln, five fascinating letters
by Warren G. Harding, a letter by Mark Twain, eight letters
by Garfield, and three dozen other choice historic papers. On
May 5, 1976, he mailed this whole collection, still tingling
from his hot fingers, to my gallery in New York.

"Wow!" I said to my assistant, as I opened the package.
"Look at this bonanza from El Dorado!" I loving caressed
each document as I took it from the huge envelope. In all
there were 45 old papers. Then, as I peered more closely at
the treasures, I noticed that the Mark Twain letter was
addressed to the California pioneer, Senator Cornelius Cole.
My mind suddenly spanned the gulf of 40 years to my student
days at U. C. L. A. and I remembered the collection of Cole
papers in the Library. Instantly I realized that I was looking at
hot merchandise and that Wade was a library thief.

I telephoned James V. Mink, the university archivist and
head of special collections. Mink's voice shook with emotion
and he was near collapse as he confirmed the theft. Mink also
informed me that, as I suspected, some of the papers I'd
received were stolen from the General Rosecrans collection at
U. C. L. A.

I gave Mink the address of Wade and told him: "You'd
better grab him right away. I think he's getting ready to blow
town."

Mink promised to contact the local cops and get a warrant
for Wade's arrest.

The next day I talked again to Mink.

He said: "I couldn't sleep last night. This whole thing's got me worried sick. Nothing like this has ever happened to us before. We've never had a theft like this."

"It's not your fault," I said. "And besides, when you capture Wade and recover the other papers he's probably got in his closet you'll be a hero.

"But," I added. "Get him fast."

The next day Mink told me that the Los Angeles constabulary refused to swear out a warrant for Wade's arrest or for the search of his residence until they had the evidence—the stolen documents sent to me—in their hands.

"Can't you get your library security officer to make the arrest?"

"No," said Mink. "He's afraid to make a move without the cops."

"Okay," I said. "I'll send you back the Mark Twain letter so you can use it as evidence. And I'll return the rest of your property as soon as you have the thief in custody."

I strongly suspected that U. C. L. A. planned to let Wade escape. Perhaps they hoped that he'd dissolve so there'd be no inquiry and the whole investigation would die out without publicity. But I knew that if U. C. L. A. let Wade off the hook, he'd simply leave town with his loot, go to another state, set up with a false moniker, and resume his filching career. I was determined to see him put behind bars. That's why I wanted to hang on to the rest of the stolen documents until he was picked up.

As all dealers and auction galleries know from acrid experience, many librarians and archivists flinch from prosecuting thieves. They don't want the publicity, and they'd rather let a thief go free and start operations elsewhere than incur the displeasure of their trustees with accusations of lax security. In my opinion a librarian or archivist who deliberately permits a thief to escape without punishment is as culpable as the criminal he abets.

Five more days passed and nothing happened. I called Mink to complain.

"The police don't feel they should act in a hasty manner," said Mink.

I screamed like an 88 shell: "Tell those Keystone Kops in L. A. to get their asses in gear or I'll turn the whole matter over to the United States postal authorities and then you'll really get some hot action out in Westwood."

Mink promised to do his best.

I was still frothing later that day when I dispatched the following telegram to Mink:

I informed you on May 10 of the removal of rare autographs from your library and supplied the name and address of the vendor. I hoped you would have him in custody by now. I also sent you by registered mail a letter of Mark Twain's which you stated you could positively identify as your property, so that you could get out a warrant for the arrest of the vendor, and I explained that I am ready to turn over to your library the balance of the papers sent to me by the vendor as soon as you furnish me with a statement holding me harmless from any legal reprisal by him. I have had no word from you. If I don't hear from you by the morning of May 19 I shall contact postal authorities here in New York so the vendor can be charged with a federal crime.

The telegram worked. In two days I got the news I was waiting for. Mink called. "We've got him," he announced. "Caught him just as he was packing to leave town. He had an open suitcase on his bed, fully packed, with a loaded revolver lying on top of his shirts. And the loot! He had some of our stuff, but there were piles of rare documents that he'd stolen in Texas—$100,000 worth, at least."

I at once returned the remainder of the stolen documents in my possession to the U. C. L. A. Library. Wade was charged with grand theft on May 20, the day of his arrest. He pleaded guilty to stealing 45 documents from the U. C. L. A. Library.

Meanwhile, the University of Texas and the Texas State Archives discovered that more than 800 letters and documents were missing from their files. Some of the papers turned up in Wade's suitcase. I rounded up a few others from my current catalog of auction offerings. Some I found were listed in an earlier sale and I managed to recover them from the purchasers and send them to the owners.

In most cases I was never compensated for returning the material, much of which I'd paid Wade for. My reward came in the letters I got from the people whom Wade had victimized. Former Governor Price Daniel of Texas wrote: "Thank you for your kindness in rescuing the letter written to me by Lyndon Johnson in 1955. I appreciate your sending it to me without cost, and I know you will beware of further consignments from that party. I have since learned that Wade had access to my papers and those of Governor Connally in the Texas State Archives." Page Ackerman, the librarian of U. C. L. A., wrote: "Your prompt and responsible action led not only to the recovery of UCLA's important material, but also may lead to the restoration of similar manuscripts to at least two archives in Texas. On behalf of the UCLA Library, I offer you our most sincere thanks. Archival collections all over the country will benefit from your prompt action."

In sentencing Wade on July 19, 1976, in Santa Monica, Judge Pierce Young cited the serious nature of the crime.

"Only the destruction of historic documents," he said, "is more heinous than their theft." Wade's sentence was a year in prison with no chance of parole and four years probation, with the proviso that he help in the recovery of the letters he'd heisted.

After Wade served his time in the Los Angeles County Jail he was taken to Texas to face charges. Judge Mace B. Thurman gave him four years probation and the admonishment: "Obey the ten commandments—especially one, and you know which one it is."

Wade said: "I will, your honor. My ambition now is to become a minister. I want to spread the gospel and drive the devil out of this world."

CHAPTER 19

A Chapter of Lists

KNIGHTS WHO ARE bold enter them; the "most
wanted" and the "best dressed" get on them; China-
men who operate laundries keep them; queens of
England announce honors in them; authors with long Russian
names compile them. What am I talking about? Lists, of
course.

I'm guilty of contributing to quite a few books of lists, but
nobody's ever asked me to draw up an auction list. A pity,
too. Auctions are such mad, glad, bad affairs—perfect for
lists!

So here, for the delectation of all afflicted with listomania,
are a few compilations.

SEVEN STRANGEST WAYS TO CONDUCT
AN AUCTION

1. Lighted-candle Auction   In secluded shires of England, it's
still the approved way to sell! The auctioneer sets up a one-
inch bit of lighted candle and takes bids until the very second
the wick falls and the light winks out. The last bidder wins
the goods.

Experienced bidders use cunning and skill in the candle
sales. They study the burning of the candle to anticipate the
final flicker. Just before the flame vanishes they yell out the
highest bid so that no one will have a chance to top it.
"When the candle is going out," wrote Samuel Pepys, who
witnessed a lighted-candle sale, "how they bawl and dispute
afterwards who bid the most first."

194

By an act of William III (1698) candle-wick auctions were prescribed for merchandise imported from the East Indies.

2. Dumb-bidding Auction   This is an English method of sale by which the seller's secret reserve is written on a slip of paper and placed beneath a flickering candle. The auctioneer then asks for bids until the candle goes out. The bid at the fall of the wick is successful only if equal to, or in excess of, the amount on the paper concealed under the candle.

3. Dutch Auction, or "Mineing"   The auctioneer calling the sale starts at a high figure, say 100 guilders, and cries his way downward to 99, 98, 97, and so on until he reaches an amount at which one of the bidders calls out: "Mine!" The lot is then sold to this bidder as the first (and only) bidder. In sophisticated circles, a sinister, ticking clock records the

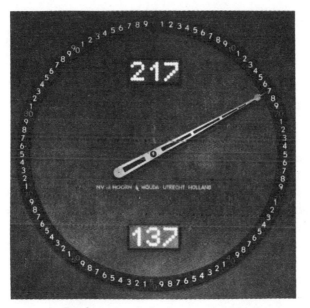

Dutch auction clock, showing price (above)
and number assigned to buyer (below)

Japanese hand-sign signals

descent of amounts until the sum reaches the maximum that any one bidder is willing to pay.

4. Japanese Hand-sign Auction   In Japanese sales, all partici-pants place their bids simultaneously by hand signals. The auctioneer glances quickly over the show of hands, reads the amounts indicated by the position of the fingers, and knocks the lot down to the highest bidder. A swift method of selling, obviating the slow rise in bidding common to American and British auctions but also eliminating a lot of the frenetic excitement.

5. Chinese Handshake Auction   An ancient form of sale by which bidders convey their secret bids to the auctioneer by a squeeze of the hand or fingers under cover of a small sheet. After each participant has "shaken hands" with the auctioneer, signaling the amount of his bid by squeezing the auctioneer's fingers a number of times in the prescribed manner, the auctioneer calls out the name of the successful bidder. This system of secret bidding makes it easy for the auctioneer to be corrupt. He can award the successful bid to a crony or confederate.

6. Whispering Auction   In this quaint type of sale, used mainly in the Orient, the bidders line up and whisper their bids in the ear of the auctioneer. Nobody knows what anyone else's bid is and the auctioneer simply knocks down the goods to the bidder with the loudest "money talks" whisper. A slow method of selling, well adapted to the soporific life in the Far East.

7. Under the Spear Auction   In ancient Rome, after every battle, the surviving Roman soldiers would auction off their loot *sub hasta* (under the spear.) Thrusting a spear into the ground as a signal that the auction was about to start, a soldier with loot would cry his own sale to assembled soldiers and civilians. Although the spear isn't used anymore, soldiers still hold private auctions. I've watched Nazi relics—pistols, medals, razors, helmets, daggers—auctioned in a tent in Belgium, even before the war ended in 1945. But food always got the biggest prices. I was present once when a corporal assembled a dozen soldiers and auctioned off a Milky Way candy bar for $5. And I was the underbidder in a crowded mess hall in France when, after spirited bidding, a slim piece of apple pie was knocked down for $10.

FOURTEEN MOST ATROCIOUS PENMEN IN HISTORY

1. Napoleon Bonaparte   Napoleon ran his words together, skipped letters here and there, rarely dotted his i's, and in general turned out such spastic chirography that some of his epistles are still undeciphered by historians. Napoleon complained: "My thoughts outrun my pen, and then goodbye to the handwriting." One French general got a letter from Napoleon and thought it was a map. Another was captured by the enemy while he was still trying to decipher Napoleon's orders to withdraw.

2. Horace Greeley   The pugnacious editor of *The New York Tribune* scrawled a hand so vile that it baffled even expert compositors. Greeley once wrote a curt note to an employee discharging him for incompetence, and for years the man used Greeley's dismissal as a letter of recommendation. Some wag commented: "If Belshazzar had seen Greeley's handwriting on the wall, he'd have been a good deal more frightened than he was." Mark Twain once got a six-word note from Greeley and worked on it three hours before he could decipher it: "Washing with soap is wholly absurd."

3. President John F. Kennedy   Kennedy's signature changed every time he wrote it. He could never make up his mind

Unreadable script of Napolean Bonaparte

whether his name was *Lummy* or *Kenning* or *Humedy*. His spelling was also pretty terrible but there is no way to prove this because his script was so bad you can never be sure of the exact way he spelled anything.

4. *Johannes Brahms* Even Germans, who scramble their participles and put verbs at the end of a sentence and are thus able to decode almost anything, can't read his handwriting. I once put a letter of Brahms's in front of a brilliant German and asked him to translate it. After ten minutes of struggle he turned the letter upside down and said: "Maybe it will make some sense this way."

5. *Elizabeth Taylor* Her signature looks like a badly tossed fishing net. If you look at it too closely you could get tangled up in it.

6. *Charles Dickens* So distinguished was the great novelist's signature that it was once reproduced in gold on the cover of each volume in his collected works. This set of his writings was known as the "Snarleo Editions" because that is precisely how most people read his creative scrawl.

7. *Mae West* This signature should be banned by the censors. The capital letters of her name are preceded by two enormous breasts that are so distracting that it's hard to concentrate on the rest of her name.

8. *J. Pierpont Morgan* A collector was once browsing through some autograph letters in my gallery. He picked one up and said: "Who signed this letter?" I said: "J. P. Morgan." "Good Lord!" he said. "I just threw out a Morgan letter yesterday. I couldn't read the signature and thought it was a forgotten vaudeville performer."

"Tom Lummy"

Very sincerely yours,

"John Kenning"

"John Humedy"

All alias John Kennedy

Elizabeth Taylor, a badly cast net

"Snarleo Editions'

(Charles Dickens)

Mae West. Two symbolic breasts

J. Pierpont Morgan

"Tired Lusts" (Frank Sinatra)

Gertrude Stein at her most legible

Walt Disney. Genuine signature

Hank Porter for Walt Disney

9. Ludwig van Beethoven His handwriting was so bad and his manuscript music so blotted and smeared that every new generation has a chance to give a fresh interpretation of what he said and the music he wrote.

10. Gertrude Stein There is a simple explanation for her strange and hard-to-understand books. No printer could make out her handwriting. I've often spent hours trying to decode a short note. But I find that no matter how I decipher her words, everybody accepts my interpretation because it always sounds the way Gertrude Stein sounds.

11. Frank Sinatra Nobody could possibly make out his signature. However, since it looks like the words "Tired Lusts," I suppose one might hazard a guess that Sinatra signed it.

12. Walt Disney The famous cartoonist's signature was so illegible that he hired a studio artist to sign his name for him.

The trademark signature that's so famous is a creation of Disney's associate, Hank Porter.

13. *Sigmund Freud* Probably the worst handwriting of any doctor who ever lived. A prescription from Freud would scare the average apothecary out of his wits. Not long ago I had a group of handwritten Freud letters that required translation. After successively frustrating a German exchange student and a professor who taught German at New York University, I placed the letters in front of a young and very clever German philographer who had just loftily informed me that *no* Gothic script posed any problem for *him*. As he bent over the first letter of Freud's a look of Teutonic bewilderment spread over his face and he uttered two words: "Mein Gott!"

14. *Louis D. Brandeis* As a Supreme Court Justice, Brandeis should have known better than to write such a terrible script. Perhaps he didn't want people to know what he was saying; if so, he succeeded, for I never saw a letter of Brandeis's in which there weren't at least two or three words that defied decipherment.

ELEVEN ZANIEST WAYS TO BID AT AUCTION

1. Cross your legs to bid; uncross them to cease bidding.
2. Move your spectacles to forehead or tip of nose to bid; replace them over your eyes to stop. (This secretive method was used by bookdealer Lew David Feldman and it was many years before even his most astute auction foe detected the signals.)
3. Unfasten the top button of your coat to bid; button it up to withdraw.
4. Pull your handkerchief partly out of your coat pocket to bid; stuff it back in to quit.
5. Hold your catalog open and pretend to read it when

bidding; close it to withdraw from fray. (A favorite method of dealers.)

6. Hold up an abacus to convey your exact raises; place it on lap to stop. (Better sit in the front row if you want to use this Oriental method.)

7. Stare steadfastly into the auctioneer's eyes to bid; avert your gaze to cease.

8. Sit down to bid; stand up to stop. (This system of signals was used by Norton Simon to buy a costly Rembrandt painting.)

9. Keep your thumb in the buttonhole of your coat to bid; take it out to stop.

10. Scratch your ear, your nose, or your head to signal a bid.

11. Or try the method used in ancient Rome and by the famed bookman, George D. Smith: just wink your eye at the auctioneer. But be careful not to get a twitch.

(If you elect to use any of these unusual methods of bidding, all of which are acceptable, be sure to clue in the auctioneer prior to the sale so that he can follow your secret signals.)

FOUR MOST UNUSUAL AUCTIONS
EVER HELD

1. The Knocking Down of the Roman Empire   In 193 A.D. the whole Roman Empire was put up for grabs by the Praetorian Guard. They'd decapitated the emperor, Pertinax (now remembered for the rarity of the coins bearing his portrait and the word *pertinaceous,* derived from his stubborn character), and put the Empire on the block to the highest bidder. Didius Julianus outbid all rivals with an offer of 6,250 drachmas (about $2,000) for every man in the imperial guard. It turned out to be a lethal purchase. Two months later the legions of Septimius Severus entered Rome and cut off the new emperor's head.

2. The Fabulous Sale of Hitler's Limousines   At an auction in Scottsdale, Arizona, in early 1973, Hitler's personal parade car, a 1940 model 770K Mercedes-Benz touring car with bulletproof doors, armor plating, and windshield glass two inches thick was knocked down for $153,000. Although the car weighed five tons, it had a 230-horsepower engine that could drive it 135 miles an hour. It got only three miles to the gallon. Another limousine of Hitler's, at the same sale, fetched $93,000. But a cheap model 1934 Ford, riddled with 200 bullet holes, that Bonnie and Clyde were driving when ambushed and gunned down by the Feds, brought an incredible $175,000, a tribute to the fascination of crime.

3. The Wild Auction of Rudolph Valentino's Effects   In August, 1926, Rudolph Valentino, only thirty-one, died of a ruptured appendix, and the women of America went mad with grief. Valentino left an estate that was only a bent sou away from bankruptcy. Every bit of his property—50 suits and over a thousand pairs of socks, with an array of rare guns, armor, weird paintings, and books—was hurriedly put on the block. Only four months after his death 2,000 lots were paraded over the podium. So desperate were the executors that they pulled all sorts of shenanigans to swindle the bidders. A Valentino bookplate had been hastily printed up and pasted in heaps of worthless books. These "association" volumes were knocked down at $3 each. A painting of Valentino as a gaucho brought $1,550. A sculpture of his hand fetched $150. Despite the immense publicity and fanfare and a sumptuous catalog the sale was a flop. The conniving sponsors took in less than $100,000.

4. The Three Incredible Sales of Lanier Washington   Lanier Washington traced his descent from Washington by a route so devious that no genealogist could ever confirm it. But despite this fugitive lineage, Lanier owned an inexhaustible supply of Washington relics that could have filled a dozen Mount Vernons. Lanier's first sale in 1917 at the Anderson Galleries (precursors of Sotheby Parke Bernet) featured 88 lots, and the biggest buyer was publisher William Randolph Hearst, looking to give a little éclat to the furnishings in San Simeon. Hearst bought for hefty prices Washington's shoe buckles, whist counters, wine glasses, coat buttons, pants, and snuffboxes. The great George D. Smith, noted bookseller and rival of A. S. W. Rosenbach, laid out $200 for a pair of Sheffield "candlesticks from Washington's desk" at Mount Vernon.

Three years later Lanier Washington held another sale at the American Art Galleries, this time offering 445 lots (he'd replenished his supply of Washington relics), all of which fetched excellent prices. Coat buttons at $125 each, shoe buckles, $370, pink seashells bought by Truthful George from an impoverished sailor, $210 each, and so on. (Another pair of Sheffield candlesticks from Washington's desk at Mount Vernon was too much for George D. Smith. After a furious argument with Lanier he dropped dead.) In 1922 the ersatz descendant of Washington held a final sale at the American Art Galleries. There were 487 lots. By this time, however, even the most obtuse dealers and credulous collectors had caught on and the prices were so ridiculously low that Lanier retired from the relic business.

TEN MOST TERRIBLE SPELLERS
IN HISTORY

1. F. Scott Fitzgerald You've got to read a letter of Fitzgerald's to believe the way he spelled. "Yatch" for "yacht," "ect." for "etc.," and so on. Even the name of his close

Wm. Shakspar   William Shaksper   William Shakspear

friend, Ernest Hemingway, he often spelled "Earnest Hem-
mingway" or "Hemmengway."

2. Marilyn Monroe She was very careful about her spelling
and often crossed out and corrected a mistake. But, on second
thought, she'd cross out the correction and replace it with the
error. Her holograph letters are filled with alterations, some
for the better, some for the worse. To the day of her death
she never made up her mind.

3. Will Rogers Either Will Rogers was an awful speller or he
was kidding the American people. He was a smart man and
very perceptive so perhaps, after all, he really knew how to
spell but didn't let on for fear it might spoil his homespun
image.

4. Israel Putnam This old Revolutionary general had two
mortal enemies: the British and his quill pen. The British
never got the better of him but the quill did. He had as much
trouble with writing as he did with spelling. The famous
soldier stuttered and I once saw a letter to which he'd signed
his name "Israel Pututnam."

5. William Shakespeare Nothing survives in Shakespeare's
writing except six signatures. How, then, can we be sure that
he was a lousy speller? Well, in the six surviving signatures he
managed to spell his own name three different ways:
Shaksper, Shakspear, and Shakspar.

6. Martha Washington   Martha was not a scholar but she was clever. She got George to write her letters for her. But now and then she penned her own notes in a crabbed script. In one letter she wrote: "Werms is the caus of all complaints in children."

7. Charles M. Russell   This great Western artist is one of the most poetic and delightful of correspondents, but his spelling passes into the realm of the unbelievable. In a letter to his author friend, Frank B. Linderman, Russell wrote: "If Scriberners like the storys its a sinch when ever thing say its ago Il start the pictures."

8. Jesse James   As James didn't have much education, it's natural he wasn't a very good speller. But he was proud of his letters and he had good reason. Nobody ever told him he was a terrible speller. People were very polite to Jesse James.

9. Nathan Bedford Forrest   This great Confederate general was notorious for his awful spelling. The few letters that survive in his hand are full of unbelievable forays into orthography. "Be the fust with the mostest" is one of his most literate comments.

10. Salvador Dali   Dali probably wrote pretty well in Spanish, his native language, but his English spelling would give Noah Webster convulsions and his fractured French, hilarious to read, would send Larousse into shock.

TEN AUCTIONED OBJECTS MOST LIKELY
TO BE FAKES

1. An original sketch by Frederic Remington   It's said that Remington turned out 2,100 sketches of which more than 4,000 are in American art galleries and museums. This figure does not include the hundreds that parade from auction to auction, year after year, seducing the unwary with forged signatures and fabricated pedigrees.

2. The Ulster County Gazette of January 4, 1800   This old newspaper announcing Washington's death on December 14, 1799, has been reprinted so many times you could blanket the entire Sovereign State of New York with the fakes. Washington's demise was stale news on January 4 to begin with, for almost every paper in the United States had printed the story before it got to Ulster County. But there's not an owner of this reprint that won't swear on the metacarpals of his ancestors that it's been in the family for over a hundred years (probably true) and that great-great-great-grandfather Hezekiah piled the copies for the printer as they came off the press (palpably false.)

3. A lock of George Washington's hair   Hair's a fragile thing. A puff of wind, a sneeze, a startled explanation, and it takes off like a bit of down. "I had a rare lock of Washington's hair," one auctioneer related, "preserved in a handsome gold locket, and I was showing it to a prospective bidder when a tiny gust of wind picked it up and carried it out the window into the street. It wasn't a serious loss, for as soon as my customer left I called in my old, colored porter and replaced the missing strands with a more copious lock."

4. The original of General Robert E. Lee's General Order No. 9 (farewell to his troops), April 10, 1865   There were scores of clerical copies of this famous farewell (actually composed by Lee's aide, Colonel Marshall), a few of them signed, but there is one "signed" copy that turns up under the gavel at least four or five times every year. That's the facsimile on blue, lined paper printed with diabolical skill by the Lakeside Press.

Every month some excited owner calls me with this historic gem.

"Is it by any chance addressed to Brigadier General Stevens?" I ask.

"Why, yes," comes the answer. "How did you know?"

And I explain tactfully (or more often not tactfully) that I'm allergic to this particular document and get a rash on my index finger if I even touch it and this allergy precludes my offering it at auction.

5. Queen Anne's chamber pot I suppose the old queen had one, but I don't think she owned the hundreds that have come up for sale at country auctions. Their pedigrees are based on hearsay: "My grandmother always told me that it once belonged to Queen Anne." There are so many such commodes around that it's unusual to find one that *didn't* belong to Queen Anne.

6. Jesse James's revolver This is the most persistent relic on the market. Even presuming that James owned an enormous arsenal and several hundred Colts and Patersons, one still can't account for the humungous number of Jesse James's pistols, *all* of them well "authenticated" with enough affidavits and I-swear-to-God's to convince a Philadelphia lawyer. Some of them even have notches on the grip, a Western-outlaw affectation promoted by Hollywood.

7. A signed, limited edition print by Picasso Why Picasso? Why not Rouault, Dali, Miro, Chagall, Norman Rockwell, or Braque? Because Picasso is the real target for fakers. My brother, Bruce, was broke in Paris in 1957 and mingled with the arty-farty crowd on the Left Bank where he consorted with some of the "specialists" who were working the American market. When he got back to New York, Bruce laid before me a group of Picasso prints, all numbered in pencil in the proper manner with as fine a Picasso signature on each as ever I saw. "I watched these being signed by a friend of mine," said Bruce. "He can do anybody, but he specializes in Picasso."

Many of these Paris fakes were personally condemned by Picasso but there are a lot of them still around. The pot-bellied artist also had a habit of writing a huge "faux" on some of his genuine, not-so-good early work that he was glad to dispose of as fraudulent.

8. A Remington bronze   Any Remington bronze must be looked over with great cunning. The more dramatic the subject the more appealing it is to the Japanese who are now turning out superb forgeries that can pass muster under all but the most jaundiced eye.

9. A pre-Columbian clay pot or a Peruvian gold effigy   Work-shops in Lima, Peru, and in Mexico City turn out spurious relics by the thousands for the American market. Especially difficult to spot are the articles in gold, since there is no way to tell old gold from new.

10. An oil painting by Raoul Dufy   For many years a dapper Hungarian named Elmyr de Hory turned his artistic bent to the production of Dufys that even before the paint was dry were eagerly bought by the world's greatest art experts. De Hory glutted the market with Dufys, then added to his wares choice examples of Matisse, Renoir, Chagall, and Modigliani. Works by all of these artists, fresh from de Hory's brush and often fortified with distinguished pedigrees, turn up constantly at auctions where the expertise is remiss.

TWELVE MOST BIZARRE ARTICLES EVER
SOLD AT AUCTION

1. Nursing bottle used by King Louis Philippe of France when an infant. Sold at Hotel Drouot in Paris in 1972 for $450.

2. Lock of hair from the mane of Robert E. Lee's warhorse, Traveller. Sold at Charles Hamilton Galleries in New York on May 28, 1981, for $110.

3. Charles Dickens' stuffed and mounted pet raven, "Grip." Sold at Gad's Hill (Dickens' home) in 1870 for 120 guineas (about $8,000 in today's money.) Grip was the "literary wonder" of the nineteenth century and inspired Dickens' novel, *Barnaby Rudge*, Poe's poem, *The Raven*, and Poe's short story, *The Purloined Letter*. Grip was acquired by the late Colonel Richard Gimbel for his Dickens and Poe collection and at his death Gimbel bequeathed the "bird of ill omen" to the Philadelphia Free Library.

4. The bottle of Scotch quaffed from by Humphrey Bogart as the alcoholic priest in **The Left Hand of God.** Sold at a Twentieth Century Fox auction in 1971 for $115.

5. Queen Victoria's bloomers. Sold at Christie's in South Kensington, England, in 1978 for $300. Victoria was a sanitation addict and changed her bloomers four times a day. She owned hundreds of plain and lace-frilled pairs.

6. Napoleon's penis. Sold at the Hotel Drouot in Paris in 1977 for $3,000. Now in the collection of a noted American urologist.

7. Joan Crawford's false eyelashes.   Sold at Plaza Galleries in New York in 1978 for $325.

8. An ancient Chinese spitoon.   Adorned with a green and yellow dragon, this rare Ming spitoon was sold at Christie's in Tokyo in February, 1980, for $145,026.

9. Gina Lollabrigida's black lace panties.   Sold at a Metro-Goldwyn-Mayer auction in May, 1970, for $30.

10. Paul Revere's anvil.   Sold at Parke-Bernet Galleries in New York in 1930 for $9,800.

11. A tooth of Sir Isaac Newton's.   Sold at Sotheby's in London in 1816 for £750 (about $20,000 in today's money). The buyer mounted it in gold and wore it as a watch fob.

12. The wig of Lawrence Sterne   (author of *Tristram Shandy*). Sold at Sotheby's in London in 1822 for 200 guineas (about $15,000 in today's money.)

TWENTY-ONE MOST EXPENSIVE ARTICLES EVER SOLD AT AUCTION

1. A hat worn by Napoleon in 1815 was sold by Maitres Liery in Rheims, France, on April 23, 1970, for $29,471, top price ever paid for a hat.

2. A Persian rug measuring 7 feet 3 inches by 12 feet 5 inches, woven in Cairo about 1500, sold at Sotheby's in London on March 29, 1978, for $229,900, highest amount ever for a carpet.

3. A snuff box of gold and lapis lazuli signed by Juste-Oreille Meissonier, dated Paris, 1728, sold at Christie's in London on June 26, 1974, for $205,475, highest sum for a snuff box.

4. A magnificent gold-hilted sword presented by the Continental Congress in 1779 to the Marquis de Lafayette sold at Sotheby Parke Bernet in New York on November 20, 1976, for $145,000, world's record for a sword.

5. A bottle of 1806 Chateau Lafite claret, one of two such bottles known, was sold at Heublein's eleventh annual National Auction of Rare Wines on May 24, 1979, in Atlanta, Georgia, for $28,000, highest price ever paid for a bottle of wine.

6. A document signed by Button Gwinnett, signer of the Declaration of Independence from Georgia, sold at Charles Hamilton Galleries in New York in October, 1979, for $100,000, world's record for an autograph.

7. A Dubois corner cabinet was sold at Sotheby's Acker-Moyer sale in Monte Carlo in 1980 for $1,800,000, greatest sum for any piece of furniture.

8. A fifteenth-century Chinese "chicken cup" (for broth) sold at Sotheby's Hong Kong in 1980 for $1,000,000, record price for a piece of china.

9. A handwritten letter by Ronald Reagan about Frank Sinatra sold at Charles Hamilton Galleries in January, 1981, for $12,500, highest price for a letter of a living person.

10. A painting by J. M. W. Turner, "Juliet and Her Nurse," was sold by Sotheby Parke Bernet in New York on May 29, 1980, for $6,400,000, top sum for any painting.

11. A poster by Toulouse Lautrec, "Moulin Rouge," sold at Phillips in New York in 1980 for $52,000, record price for a poster.

12. A 36-page manuscript by Leonardo da Vinci on cosmology sold at Christie's in London on December 12, 1980, for $2,200,000, world's record for a manuscript.

13. A photograph of Alexandre Dumas by Felix Nadar taken in 1857 was sold on November 2, 1979, for $16,000, highest amount ever fetched for a single photograph image.

14. A unique British Guiana one cent stamp issued in 1856

sold at Sotheby Parke Bernet in New York in the spring of 1980 for $935,000, greatest sum ever fetched by a rare stamp.

15. A Brasher doubloon, a gold coin minted in New York by Ephraim Brasher of which only seven are known, sold at Bowers and Ruddy in New York on November 29, 1979, for $725,000, highest amount ever brought by a rare coin.

16. A painting by Frederick E. Church, "The Icebergs," was knocked down at Sotheby Parke Bernet in New York in November, 1979, for $2,500,000, greatest amount for any American painting.

17. A print by Mary Cassatt, "Woman Bathing," was sold at Sotheby Parke Bernet in New York in February, 1980, for $72,000, a world's record for a print.

18. A copy of the Gutenberg Bible, first book ever printed from movable type, was sold by Christie's in New York on April 7, 1978, for $2,000,000, highest price for a rare book.

19. A painting by Rubens, "Samson and Delilah," was knocked down at Christie's in London on July 11, 1980, for $5,400,000, biggest amount ever fetched for an Old Master.

20. A photograph by Ansel Adams, "Moonrise, Hernandez, New Mexico," was sold at Christie's in New York on October 31, 1979, for $15,000, record price for a twentieth-century photograph.

21. A 1936 Mercedes-Benz roadster sold to a telephone bid from Monaco at Christie's sale in Los Angeles on February 25, 1979, for $421,040, top sum ever paid for a used car.

CHAPTER 20

The Thrills of Auction Bidding

T HE FIRST TIME you attend an auction you may be amazed by its explosive speed. Invisible bids fly at the auctioneer and his spotters from every part of the salesroom. You may wonder how you can take part in any battle so swift and subtle, with floor bidders often as crafty and elusive as Indians, signaling their bids by the crook of a finger or a flip of their spectacles and at times dodging behind pillars or retreating almost out of the gallery so that their competitors will not suspect they're taking part in the fray.

"The first time I ever bid," one of my customers told me, "I didn't know what to expect and I was scared, really scared. But after I'd bought a couple of lots I could tell when the auctioneer had his eye on me. I began to enjoy it enormously. By the end of the sale I felt like I'd had a valium. It took me an hour to recover from the sheer intoxication."

It's the world's most exhilarating game, this skirmish of wits between you and the auctioneer. Great prizes are won or lost in a few seconds. Often the excitement is so intense you can hear the gasps and sighs from the audience and the bidders. There may be a sudden stirring, an undulation of heads and a craning of necks as the rapier thrusts of the combatants are spurred on by the man at the podium.

The thrill of an auction begins with the pre-sale exhibit, open to everyone. It's like having the run of a great museum where every item is for sale. You can see and touch and hold great treasures. The gold of the ancient Incas or the silver of the Spanish Main will gleam in your hands. You can sit in carved oak chairs where once great courtiers parked their velvet pantaloons. You can relish the crackle of old parchment and hold the mellowing letters by Napoleon and Lincoln, Dickens and Whitman. You can walk on lush Kirman carpets that caress your ankles. You can gaze upon original paintings of the great masters, even reach out and fondle the glowing colors.

All that is beautiful and rare from mankind's past will be yours for a few moments. And you will sooner or later acquire a rich knowledge that cannot be got in any university.

At even the most posh sales the doors are open to you to watch and enjoy the auction without bidding. Except on very rare occasions, you need no money, no ticket, no identification, no credentials. A love of excitement will get you through the doors. You'll find that watching an auction in action is a lot like watching players in a gambling casino. If you're bereft of pelf you can have a wonderful time just observing the madness of the participants, the faces of the gamblers intent upon victory, the cries of joy or fury, the greed or wildness in the eyes. You'll be regaled for an afternoon or evening and not spend a cent.

The first time you go to an auction sale, if it is a leisurely one, you may not perceive the intrigue that deepens in direct ratio to the rarity and value of the lot being sold and the assets of those who are bidding for it. Some participants feign indifference, then suddenly burst in with their bids, hoping to intimidate or discourage their opponents and put them to rout. Others violently probe the air with their pencils. Many bid furtively with eye-winks, twitches, or adjustments of the necktie. A few lose their nerve and wilt in the face of the enemy. Others grow in audacity as the action gets madder and brazenly cry out their bids.

Some avid competitors hide their identities under weird

sobriquets. A world-famed urologist usually bids under the number "69." Once a notorious dealer whom I knew to be dishonest stole from my gallery a scarce book on philography by Thomas Madigan. At my auction sale the next day he smiled sardonically as he bid under the alias "Madigan," openly boasting about his theft from me.

Exciting struggles, verging on brawls, often break out in the salesroom. Tempers are stoked to a blaze in the fury of bidding. One of the most dramatic auctions ever held was the last sale I conducted at the once-elegant Gotham Hotel in New York. There'd been a lot of pre-sale publicity because I was offering at the same sale letters of Jacqueline Kennedy and Lee Harvey Oswald, a quite accidental juxtaposition that delighted historians and horrified sentimentalists. Jackie was then the adored madonna of the press and the multitude, not yet "tarnished" by her marriage to Onassis. An affront to Jackie was an insult to American womanhood and martyred greatness.

My salesroom was crowded with bidders, spectators, reporters and cameramen. There was a plump woman in blue eyeshadow who had come to heckle. When the letters of Oswald were put on the block—they fetched a total of $7,165—she rose dramatically, faced the television cameras, and orated in a voice loud enough to fracture the chandeliers: "I wouldn't give you a dollar for them." At the time I thought perhaps she did not have a dollar to give, but later I learned from a reporter that she was a professional heckler who specialized in disrupting stockholder meetings.

The Gotham Hotel also decided to get a piece of the action by passing out circulars in the ballroom they had rented to me:

The Gotham Hotel management doesn't approve of Charles Hamilton auctioning the Mrs. Jacqueline

Kennedy and Lee Harvey Oswald letters. The hotel considers their being auctioned in bad taste. It wasn't aware they would be auctioned when Mr. Hamilton rented the ballroom.

A television newscaster asked me for a comment on the Gotham Hotel's circular.

"If they were as eager to improve their service as they are to improve my taste," I said, "they'd have a great hotel."

After the auctioneer had cried his last lot and the lights of the great chandeliers were dimmed, a disgruntled collector, unsuccessful in his bids, approached me and snarled: "That wasn't an auction, Hamilton. It was a circus."

"You're quite right," I answered. "And if I'd known how exciting it was going to be, I'd have sold ringside tickets."

In my auction at the Waldorf-Astoria on January 22, 1981, an exact duplicate of Nixon's letter of resignation from the presidency was cataloged for sale. At the request of members of the media, I advanced its position in the sale and sold it early. It was knocked down to Alan Shawn Feinstein, an investment expert from Rhode Island, at the price of $6,250.

When the auctioneer subsequently reached the number in the sale from which the Nixon had been extracted, and announced that the document was sold earlier, a man in the audience cried out: "I came here to bid on that! I demand that you put it up for sale again."

The auctioneer was tactful but firm in his refusal, pointing out that the terms of sale permitted him to change the order of selling lots at his discretion. But the man continued to rage, shaking his fist in fury. "This auction is crooked," he shouted. "You pulled a fast one on me. I've been cheated!"

"You'll have to leave, sir," said the auctioneer.

By now the audience had joined the brouhaha.

"Get out!" someone yelled.

"Beat it!"

"Show him the door!"

Finally, blustering and cursing and even threatening some of the audience, the would-be bidder retreated from the salesroom.

There was a happy ending to this exciting encounter. The next day the wild man calmed down and bought the Nixon resignation from Feinstein for $10,000. Since I had estimated the value of the original resignation at $100,000 in a list of "the most valuable autographs" I'd prepared for *The Book of Lists*, perhaps the document was a bargain at $10,000.

THE WHITE HOUSE

WASHINGTON

August 9, 1974

Dear Mr. Secretary:

I hereby resign the Office of President of the United States.

Sincerely,

The Honorable Henry A. Kissinger
The Secretary of State
Washington, D.C. 20520

Richard Nixon resigns! An exact copy of the most famous document of modern times, signed in full by Nixon. Sold at Hamilton Galleries, 1981, $6,250

Every auction has its comic moments. A bidder in one of the big galleries in New York lost his wallet during the excitement of the sale. He spoke privately to the auctioneer, who announced: "A wallet containing $2,000 has been lost in this room. The owner is offering a reward of $200 for its return."

"$225" came a reward bid from the rear.

Once a very attractive young lady with a tiny baby entered my gallery during the bidding and found a seat on the aisle. Her beauty vaguely registered on me, but I was so taken up with the problems of the sale that I had no chance to cast an eye in her direction. After the auction was over, a dour old woman approached me. "That woman with the little baby," she said, "had the unmitigated nerve to breast-feed her child during the sale, right in front of everybody."

"I'm shocked," I said. "The next time you see anything like that at one of my sales, let me know and I will look into it at once."

I hope you will come to love the thrills and madness, the infinite pleasures in a little room that are the lot of the auction goer. Visit a sale and watch for yourself. Above all, don't be hesitant to join in the struggle for heirlooms. My wife Diane and I have furnished our apartment in New York and our country home in Westhampton Beach with antiques and paintings bought at auction, and they are today worth triple what we paid for them four or five years ago. If we'd bought our furniture and decorative items new, they'd be second-hand merchandise worth but a fraction of what they cost us.

My advice to all who long for drama and excitement, and who love the beautiful and rare, is to proceed forthwith to the nearest auction gallery. Enjoy the bidding as a spectator sport for a while, then take a crack as a competitor. But be wary! You may find it a sport so exhilarating that it turns into a lifetime addiction.

CHAPTER 21

How to Control the Auctioneer: 13 Rules for Bidders

G O INTO THE auction room with the attitude that you're in charge. Without you there wouldn't be a sale. You're paying the money and the auctioneer's job is to serve you. An air of calm superiority is especially important in dealing with a huckster who speaks British. Keep in mind that he is in America only by your sufferance. Do not hold the fact that he can't speak English against him, but insist that he accord you all the courtesy and privileges due you as an American citizen.

Here are 13 rules that will help you keep the auctioneer under control:

Rule 1. Study the terms of sale carefully. These are the terms printed in front of the catalog, often in fine print. The finer the print the more carefully you should examine the sale terms. Make sure you are familiar with each of the terms before you bid. "I once lost a marvelous old painting at a sale," a friend told me, "because I let the auctioneer re-open the bidding after he'd knocked the lot down to me at a bargain price. Somebody yelled out: 'Hey, I was bidding on that!' So the auctioneer started the bidding again, and the price shot way up and I lost out. Later I discovered that the moment that the auctioneer's hammer falls the property is legally mine. This fact is clearly stated in the catalog terms of sale."

Rule 2. Don't put much confidence in the catalog estimates of value.   Sometimes the pre-sale estimates are ridiculously low because the gallery is ignorant of the rarity or desirability of what it's selling. Sometimes they're preposterously high because a greedy consignor has forced the gallery to put a big reserve on his lots, thus necessitating high estimates. Often, too, a big reserve is put on a lot in order to knock off a certain mark, perhaps a collector who will bid only on very expensive material and won't touch any lot with an estimate of less than ten or twenty thousand dollars.

Rule 3. Examine the lots that interest you before the sale. Chances are the auctioneer knows nothing at all about what he's selling and this gives you the upper hand. Read up on the lots that you hope to buy. The more you know the luckier you'll get. Unless you're convinced that the auction gallery is honest and every item is strictly as described and unconditionally guaranteed, be wary about bidding on anything you haven't examined. If the auctioneer mis-describes a lot, or if he doesn't realize its importance, that's your good luck. As a bidder you have no obligation to inform him if he makes a blunder. Seize any advantage he offers you!

Rule 4. Keep track of the lot numbers carefully and don't bid on the wrong lot.   If anyone gets mixed up, make sure it's the auctioneer and not you. At a recent Phillips sale I bid with great zeal on two old percussion rifles that I hoped to buy as ornaments for the walls of my country home. To my great delight they were knocked down to me at a fraction of their value. But when I went to the desk to pick them up, I discovered that I had, by mistake, bought a stuffed finch under a glass dome. I was so embarrassed by my folly that I pretended I wanted it. I paid for the bird (evidently taxidermized during molting season!) and hid it in my closet under a pile of clothes, hoping that my wife wouldn't discover that I'd invested sixty dollars in an inedible fowl. Of course, Diane found it. She quietly displayed it prominently in our dining room and told all our friends about my mistake. There it perches, even now, a Victorian relic that should have been pitched out when the old queen died. Whenever our friends come to visit, they comment on the mildewing bird and laugh and slap their thighs and point the finger of scorn at me.

Rule 5. Don't let the auctioneer infect you with bidder's fever. At an auction where the bidding is slow, or the audience is small or lethargic, the auctioneer may use you as a live sucker to work up some preliminary action. He may also try to stampede you by talking with great rapidity and pointing at you as the bids mount with increasing speed. Simmer him down by waiting a few moments before giving him a nod or a raised hand. Remember that speed from the auctioneer is good for the gallery but bad for you. At a dishonest sale, the auctioneer may try to "run" you, or force you up by taking bids from a shill or off the wall. Keep him under control by slowing him down and curbing his zest.

Rule 6. Remain calm at all times.   If the auctioneer wants to get worked up, or pretend to get worked up, let him. It's his privilege. But keep in mind that you're the buyer and he's the seller. Let your slogan be: "The buyer is always right." If you have a tendency to lose your cool in the heat of battle, pay a dealer a ten-percent commission to execute your bids for you and sit next to him or near him during the sale. Or, follow the method of Edmond de Goncourt, the noted French author and connoisseur, who confessed: "There's only one way I can escape the terrible tension of any auction: I read my copy of Plato until the critical moment of bidding." Or, if you trust the gallery, submit your bids by mail. Most of the great auction houses and many of the smaller ones will use your mail bids competitively and you may, at times, buy an article for much less than the amount of your bid. Another advantage to mail bids is that when a mail bid is tied with a floor bid, the mail bid (being the earlier one) wins the lot.

Rule 7. Stick to your pre-sale limit.   Before you enter the auction salesroom, make sure that you write in your catalog the amount of your bid limits. Never exceed them in the madness of the sale. The auctioneer may try with soft, coaxing words to beguile you into going a little higher but resist his blandishments. "One more bid," he may say, with a reassuring little smile. Or, "We're just getting started. Are you going to quit now?" with an air of disappointment. Or: "A beautiful painting. Worth more, much more." Resist temptation and stop when you reach your pre-sale limit.

Rule 8. Never fear the auctioneer.   Don't let him stare you down and don't let him bully you. If you want to scratch your nose, do it. If you want to wave to a friend, do so. And, should the auctioneer be so obtuse as to misinterpret your gestures and say, "Are you bidding?" merely shake your head. There is no need for you to be embarrassed because the auctioneer can't tell a head scratcher from a bidder.

Rule 9. Watch the auctioneer carefully at all times.   Don't let your mind wander unless you are in the salesroom just as a spectator. Above all, don't be distracted by the activities of bidders around you. Otherwise you may miss an important bid. Sometimes the auctioneer himself gets confused and sells a lot out of order. This always works to the disadvantage of sleepy or inattentive bidders. If you are alert you may acquire an important item for a fraction of its value.

Rule 10. Never give the auctioneer any clue to your interest. If you chat with the auctioneer about any lot before or during the sale, you will thus inform him that you're interested and he may be tempted to run you up. If you point out to the auctioneer that there are defects in the merchandise he's about to offer—a chip, a crack, a tear, a repair, a scratch, a missing knob—he will instantly realize that you want the lot and may take advantage of your interest. By pointing out a defect you may double the price you have to pay.

Rule 11. Never jump in after the bidding on a lot has cooled down. Many "experienced" bidders will tell you it's a good idea to let the bidding on a desirable lot run its course until only two lackadaisical bidders are left in the competition, then step in with a sudden, fresh bid and grab the lot. That's a crock. You are very apt to revive the interest of earlier bidders and even bring in other new bidders. If you pitch in a late bid, the auctioneer will cry out gleefully, "Fresh blood!" or, perhaps, "A new country heard from!" And he will seize upon your bid to rouse the whole floor to action. Many a lot, about to be knocked down for a fraction of its value, has been revived at the last moment by a new bidder and ended up fetching two or three times its actual worth.

Rule 12. After the sale is over and you pick up the lots you've bought, be sure to examine each lot carefully. Make certain the auctioneer or the gallery hasn't pulled a fast one on you. The lot should be exactly as described in the catalog or by the auctioneer. It's at this point in your transaction that you may be swindled unless you're dealing with a reliable gallery. Horror stories about auction houses of ill repute are common: switches in merchandise, compotes offered without covers, steins without lids or handles, couches without cushions, chairs without legs, porcelain with fresh cracks or cracks covered by pasted-on labels—almost every calamity that any antiquity or painting is heir to. "The worst part of making an auction purchase," one oldtime collector told me, "is when you pick up your lots. Sometimes I have a big row over what I've bought. And once in a while I even have to threaten legal action before I can get exactly what the auctioneer sold me."

Rule 13. Sharpshoot the sale.   If it's bargains you're after, and who isn't, be prepared at any moment to pitch in a bid on any lot that's going for a ridiculously low price. The moment you see the auctioneer is in trouble and unable to get a bid, alert yourself for the kill. Don't be one of those lugubrious chumps who, after the auction sale is over and the prizes are carried off, laments: "Golly, if I'd known it was going to go so cheaply, I'd have bid on it."

If you've ever made that remark, then pay special attention to this rule.

One of my closest friends, the late Robert K. Black of New Jersey, always attended my auctions prepared for sharpshooting. He never passed up a bargain. Once I saw him make a private sale in my gallery only seconds after the auctioneer's hammer fell on the final lot. As he was taking a check from his customer, I said: "What was that you just sold?"

"Why," said Bob, "it was the collection of Civil War soldier's letters that you had estimated at $650."

"What did you pay for the lot?" I asked, as I had been too busy during the sale to keep track of the prices.

"Three hundred. Just turned it over for $450 to this gentleman here."

Then I asked Bob: "Did you come prepared to bid on those letters?"

"No; I hadn't any intention of bidding on them. But they

were going so cheaply I realized they were a great bargain. I just pitched in a bid and got lucky."

An alert sharpshooter may also pick up a "sleeper," or rarity unidentified as such, now and then. On June 3, 1980, one of my customers, Gary Grossman, was a spectator at Sotheby Parke Bernet's sale of the last part of the great collection of Philip D. Sang. The following lot came up for bids:

> 947. KENNEDY, JOHN F. Two typed letters signed ("Jack"), one with autograph subscription, 2 pages, 4to, Palm Beach, Florida, and Congress, 10 December 1946 and 22 June 1948, to Mrs. Kay Thom, thanking her for congratulations on his election as a congressman and for her condolences on the death of his sister Kathleen, one with envelope * Together with a telegram from Kennedy to Mrs. Thom, an invitation to his wedding to Jacqueline Bouvier, two envelopes bearing his printed franking signature as Senator, two snapshots of Kennedy in naval uniform with two companions, and another item.
> Together 10 pieces. Estimate $500/$600.

The auctioneer was fighting to get a bid. Since there were two letters of Kennedy in the lot, Grossman raised a finger at $250 and the lot was knocked down to him.

"I never planned to buy that lot or any lot," he told me later. "But the price was so low I just stepped in and took it. After all, I figured that I couldn't lose. Two John F. Kennedy letters for $125 each—ridiculous!"

The room was filled with experts—dealers and collectors—when Grossman made his purchase.

A few weeks after the sale, Gary brought the collection to me and asked: "Can you sell all of it except the wedding invitation and the letter by John F. Kennedy about his election to Congress? Maybe I can get my investment back on the other stuff and have the letter I'm keeping for nothing."

"You can do a lot better than that," I told him. "Just leave the stuff with me for research and cataloging and I'll get you a good price for it."

I had instantly recognized the document described by Sotheby Parke Bernet as "another item" as the original message for help sent out by Kennedy and his men after PT-109 was rammed by a Jap destroyer in the Solomon Islands. As historians know, it was not the coconut carved by Kennedy that brought the rescuers, but this note scribbled by Ensign L. J. Thom on the back of a ragged invoice issued by a Solomon Islands tobacconist.

I sold the second Kennedy letter, the one Grossman didn't

Message sent by John F. Kennedy's marooned crew of PT-109.
Sold by Hamilton Galleries, 1980, $4,400

want, for $425 at my September 18, 1980, sale at the Waldorf, nearly double the amount that Gary had paid for the entire collection three months earlier.

As for the message written by Ensign Thom, a rat-gnawed bit of paper that Sotheby Parke Bernet had regarded as worthless and that had cost Gary nothing, it fetched a resounding $4,400.

I hope that you, too, will use the sharpshooting technique to pick up great bargains. And, if you are lucky, perhaps you may get a sleeper worth a hundred or more times what it costs you.

In any event, if you follow my 13 rules carefully you will thwart the auctioneer and beat him at his own game.

CHAPTER 22

A Blueprint for
the Future of Auctions

W ELL, I'VE SOLD my stock in Parke-Bernet and got out," said Colonel Richard Gimbel.

"How come?" I asked. "I thought you were mighty keen on that company. You sure rallied to their defense whenever I had a little spat with them."

"The British have taken over," said Gimbel. "I don't like the British. I wouldn't invest a counterfeit farthing in a British firm."

I knew why. Gimbel had been a colonel in the airforce when I was a sergeant. We'd never met then, but we both knew that the British antiaircraft gunners used to fire "by accident" on American planes when they came limping back from raids on the Nazis. The British never made this "mistake" when our aircraft were on their way to the target loaded with bombs. It was only when they were coming home, their ailerons shot away, or an engine knocked out, or the hydraulic lines cut by flak, or with wounded or dead men aboard. That's when the British gunners got their jollies by peppering us—when our planes were too beat up even to take evasive action.

For a while after Richard made the remark about not liking the British he and I just sat in silence. Gimbel was toying with a copy of my latest auction catalog, sort of flipping through the pages.

"Does the British takeover change your position in any way?" he said, alluding to my newly established gallery, only a year old in 1964.

"I don't think so," I said. "I presume they'll keep on doing what Parke-Bernet was doing."

"Don't you think they're a little bit vulnerable right now? Over-extended, maybe?"

I didn't answer because I could tell from Gimbel's expression that he was thinking out loud. He'd been the big shot of Gimbel's Department Store and was a wary old crow when it came to business economics.

"I got eight million dollars from the sale of my stock," said Gimbel.

"With eight million dollars I could strip the flesh off their bones," I said.

"Yeah?"

"Yeah. And then crack their bones and suck the marrow out."

"And how would you do all this?" asked Gimbel.

"Well, Richard, you've got my auction credo right in the catalog you're holding. Read it, and you'll see that I'm already doing a lot of important things for my customers that Parke-Bernet doesn't do."

The credo I referred to had got a lot of attention in the press because the whole idea of it was new to the auction world. It read:

AN AMERICAN AUCTIONEER'S CREDO

I believe that . . .

1. An auction house has the same ethical obligations as any other business.

2. An auction house should handle only merchandise which it can expertize and unconditionally guarantee. To offer merchandise "as is" or "at the buyer's risk"

reflects upon the integrity of the auction house and upon the intelligence of the bidder.

3. Consignment rates should be reasonable and fair, scaled according to the estimated value of the merchandise.

4. All consigned lots should be sold or cataloged within a maximum of three months from the date of consignment.

5. An auction house should never "chase hearses" or plunder the obituary columns, thus pressuring executors into a decision during a period of sorrow and confusion.

6. Pre-sale estimates should be printed in every auction catalog—not provided separately or at an additional charge.

7. An auction house should be honest in its appraisals, never offering exaggerated estimates to obtain important consignments.

8. An auction house should discourage consignment reserves because they inhibit the auction function of unrestricted sale, deceive prospective buyers, and often establish false or misleading values.

9. If a consignor insists on a reserve the amount should be published in the auction catalog in place of the estimate; and if the lot fails to fetch the reserve, it should be recorded officially as "passed."

10. The name of neither consignor nor buyer should be revealed unless by his request.

11. Every lot should be cataloged carefully, in as much detail as possible, and if there are any defects they should be carefully noted.

12. The cataloger should be not only an expert in his field but also a skilled writer who knows how to emphasize the significant features in every lot.

13. All bids submitted by mail, phone, or in person

prior to the auction should be held in strictest secrecy to
be used competitively during the sale.

"Now," I went on, "Parke-Bernet guarantees nothing.
They don't print estimates in the catalog. Everything they
sell has got a secret reserve. They manage to beat the hearse
to the corpse every time. They hold material for years,
sometimes, before selling it. They run a mighty loose
operation and are ripe to be plucked. A well-organized
gallery, built entirely on ethical bases and conducted like a
regular retail gallery, could put them on the skids in a year. I
personally know experts in almost every field who would be
delighted to work with us.

"With eight million dollars we could take them with ease,
with ease, Richard."

"Would you like to run such a gallery?" asked Gimbel.

"I don't know," I said. "Let me give it some thought."

Gimbel had offered me a chance to change the whole
history of auctioneering, a chance to put my ideas into
practice on a vast scale. It was the most tempting offer I'd
ever had, but the whole concept had one serious flaw and that
flaw was Richard Gimbel's temperament. I knew him pretty
well, well enough to swap neckties with him after a few drinks
at the Yale Club. Gimbel was used to running the show and
so was I. If I became president of the new firm, I'd pay a
prohibitive tariff of constant suggestions, reminders, reproofs,
and nagging from Gimbel.

I knew I couldn't succeed without complete authority,

especially the authority to make instant decisions without
consulting anyone.

And so, in the end, I turned Gimbel down. Several years
later he collapsed and died suddenly. To the very end he
cherished the hope of humbling the growing might of
Sotheby Parke Bernet.

In the decade since Richard Gimbel died Sotheby Parke
Bernet has made great strides toward becoming Amer-
icanized. They have jettisoned many of the ancient British
practices that made people wary of auctions. They have
introduced a modified guarantee on the goods they offer, as
has Christie's. They now print pre-sale estimates in the
catalog, although on separate pages so they are difficult to
consult during the sale. But they still have a long way to go.

Which brings me to the question often put to me: "What is
the future of auctioneering in America?"

Only last week I talked with an old collector about the
growing problems posed by the successful conquest of America by the great British auction firms. I pointed out:

"Americans now accept without dismay the fact that the
British run the auction world in New York. They are properly
subservient in the presence of a British accent. They accept
snobbery as a way of life.

"Sotheby and Christie's are backed by enormous capital
and are firmly entrenched in America. Their skilled lobbyists
are primed to prevent any legal encroachment or curb on
their activities."

"You mean they're going to swallow up all American
competition?"

"They've already devoured their rivals," I said. "They now
lead Americans by the nose. Sotheby and Christie's set the
taste in collecting. They have the power to alter fashions in
art and trends in literature. It's an immense power they

possess. You might almost say that they hold in their hands the cultural future of America."

"Surely there's something we can do about it."

"In my opinion," I continued, "one of two things, or both of them, will happen. Either Sotheby will buckle under its own weight—it's very vulnerable to a bad recession—or the Department of Consumer Affairs that now slumbers will awaken and force the great British firms to conform to the ethical standards of the United States.

"The first thing that the Department of Consumer Affairs should do is make the secret reserve illegal and compel every auction house, British and American, to print in its catalog, next to every lot, the exact amount of the reserve on it.

"The second thing they should do is force every auction gallery to guarantee what it sells. The great auction houses in New York should be reputable firms, willing to stand without cavil or restrictions behind the merchandise they sell. Their guarantees should be full and unqualified."

My old friend agreed with me. But there are some other things, too, that I think would help to secure the future of auctioneering as a great American indoor sport.

When auction galleries own material (rather than having it consigned) they are tempted to pull bids off the chandeliers. A law forcing auction houses to indicate in their catalogs by asterisk or dagger what material they own would enormously help to curb the abuses that spring from the auctioneer's private ownership of merchandise. Bidders are entitled to know when the gallery is selling its own property and the reserves are the gallery's own buy-in prices.

It should be required, also, of all galleries that they set the date or approximate date of the auction in which consigned lots will be sold. This information should be written into the contract. More than three years ago I consigned a few lots to

Sotheby Parke Bernet and, although they have sold several of them, there remain several as yet uncataloged and unsold. Three years is a long time to wait for a consignment to be sold at what is euphemistically termed "a suitable sale." The big galleries yield only to date-giving when engaged in a savage competition for desirable material with other galleries. If you consign a collection of modest value you are at the mercy of the gallery's whims.

The auction galleries in America already pose a serious threat to private dealers and this threat is growing day by day. It seems to me that the sanctuary for any menaced business, whether it be auction or retail, lies in honesty and ethics.

CHAPTER 23

A Glance at
New York's Galleries

NEW YORK IS THE auction hub of the world. It is the vortex into which is drawn all that is beautiful and precious, put on the block for the highest bidder. It is the podium from which the rare and costly and sometimes the tawdry and ersatz are knocked down. When the gavel falls in New York the rap is heard around the world.

Here, in the toyland of grownups, you can find at public sale whatever you seek. If there is nothing you seek, the serendipity that is everywhere in this great city will guide you to something you've always secretly longed for.

Of the scores of auction galleries in New York there are only about 15 of importance that deal in any form of fine art. All of them I recommend.

SOTHEBY PARKE BERNET
980 Madison Avenue (fine arts)
1334 York Avenue (decorative arts)
171 East 84th Street (books, stamps, and coins)
This mighty enterprise constantly flexes its conglomerated muscle in the art world. Its influence, good or baneful, is immense. But once you enter the gallery on Madison Avenue jettison all doubts, wink at the snobbery, and relish the sumptuous beauty of the decor and the lushness of the exhibitions. Here, in the great salesrooms on the third floor,

is knocked down everything that is fine and choice and sought by connoisseurs, whether paintings of the masters or the moderns, Oriental rugs, or beautiful jewels. The handsome and beautifully illustrated catalogs will guide you to the exhibits and the sales. If you love the excitement of public vendue, these great galleries may turn out to be your headquarters.

CHRISTIE'S
502 Park Avenue
and
CHRISTIE'S EAST
219 East 67th Street.

If you are prepared to overlook their snobbery, Christie's is an elegant and fascinating gallery at which to window shop and to buy. The aspiring socialite will make Brownie points by displaying their latest and most opulent catalog on his or her coffee table. For paintings and porcelains, carpets and jewelry, Christie's is unsurpassed. The glories of the earth pass through their hands and, if you are rich, they can pass right into yours. But even if no oil gushers have erupted on your terrace, you can still find many wonderful buys at bargain prices.

PHILLIPS, SON AND NEALE
867 Madison Avenue and 525 East 72nd Street

The smallest of the three British invaders is still snobbish enough to sport among its employees a few elevated noses. But as the largest privately owned gallery in the world, it offers a vast variety of choice items for the collector in every field—furniture, stamps, paintings, prints, old silver, carpets, African tribal masks. All the things that make for a luxurious and beautiful world may be examined at their exhibitions and bought at fair prices, sometimes bargain prices.

WILLIAM DOYLE GALLERIES
175 East 87th Street

This relatively new gallery, already one of the greatest in the city, teems with vitality and life. It is a madhouse during the exhibition and crowded at the sales. On Sunday, when other galleries are shut down, it's a perfect place to browse for an hour or two if you don't mind the melee. The variety of material offered varies from the irresistibly tempting to the readily resistible. But the owner, William Doyle, is progressive and alert and always assembles a fascinating collection of rare and choice heirlooms.

TEPPER GALLERIES
110 East 25th Street

Here you will find a wild jumble of odds and ends, always with many lots that will intrigue you. Whatever you're looking for, from mirrors to bedsteads, from antique radios to rare vases and handsome paintings, you may find here. The attendants are courteous and the range of values will appeal to the modestly heeled collector or young couple furnishing an apartment.

MANHATTAN GALLERIES
1415 Third Avenue (at 80th Street)

The impression you will get during the pre-sale exhibit is one of disorientation, but you will run across many interesting lots. As with the other medium-priced galleries, the mimeographed catalog is free and devotes only a few words to each lot, but the attendants will answer questions. The variety offered is enormous, from paintings and rugs to eye-catching odds and ends and cartons of books, anything that's ever beeen collected or ever will be collected. An excellent gallery at which to browse and buy.

LUBIN GALLERIES
30 West 26th Street
A sort of glorified flea market, this modest gallery is a catchall for inexpensive and occasionally very choice antiquities. Decorative items abound, and lots of silver, old prints, books, china, and other items, often of fairly modern vintage, are their specialty. A pleasant place in which to browse and buy.

ASTOR GALLERIES
1 West 39th Street
Less costly heirlooms abound here, with a mighty array of furniture and silver, china, and decorative artifacts. Occasionally a rare and choice item turns up and, should it pass unnoticed by experts, it may become yours for a fraction of its value. An excellent viewing and buying gallery for newlyweds.

SPECIALTY GALLERIES

SWANN GALLERIES
140 East 25th Street
An auction emporium of scarce and desirable books, this long-established gallery attracts the bids of bibliophiles from all over the country. Its weekly catalogs are accurate and can be relied upon. In addition to books, Swann offers autographs, old prints, rare maps, and photographica.

STACK'S
123 West 57th Street
America's leading numismatist, Stack's conducts frequent auctions of rare coins, American and foreign, modern and ancient. Their beautifully illustrated catalogs should be in the library of every coin collector. Even the beginner can venture

a bid or two at their sales, which, incidentally, include also the world's most precious coins.

BERNARD D. HARMER
6 West 48th Street

A giant among stamp auctioneers, this gallery issues sumptuous reference catalogs and offers for sale the finest and most dazzling array of rarities.

ROBERT A. SIEGEL
120 East 56th Street

A gallery widely recognized as the largest philatelic auction house in America. Their sales are exciting and their catalogs are handsome, especially the catalog for their incomparable "Rarities of the World" sale, held once a year.

JOHN C. EDELMANN GALLERIES
123 East 77th Street

Specialists in rugs and tapestries, this new gallery is *the* place to look at and buy choice Oriental carpets. They are knowledgeable, courteous, pleasant, and will go far out of their way to be of help to viewers or buyers.

HARMER ROOKE NUMISMATISTS, LTD.
3 East 57th Street,
6th Floor

Their beautiful coin auction catalogs are loaded with choice offerings. A visit to Harmer Rooke can be a provocative and thrilling experience, for they also specialize in Greek, Roman, Egyptian, and Mayan antiquities, as well as autographs. Their occasional auction sales of antiquities are exciting, full of unusual historic treasures.

CHARLES HAMILTON GALLERIES
25 East 77th Street
The world's largest auction firm specializing in autographs and manuscripts, with sales of more than 50,000 letters and documents every year at the Waldorf-Astoria.

CHAPTER 24

Glossary of Auction Terms

Appraisal Evaluation of an article or group of articles to be sold at auction. The usual charge for an auction appraisal ranges from no charge to $1,000, depending upon the value and number of the articles included in the appraisal.

Bidder's fever A harmless but expensive ailment common to habitués of the auction gallery.

Bid-in Same as *buy-in* or *reserve.*

Big bid ploy A fraudulent method of bluffing bidders out of the action by spreading false rumors that one or more lots will fetch a very high price, so it's useless to bid on them.

Block The auctioneer's podium.

Book The record of absentee or proxy bids, usually received by mail or telephone, kept by the gallery and used competitively by the auctioneer against floor bidders at the sale.

Buy-back Lot purchased at an auction sale by the owner.

Buyer rings See *rings.*

Buyer's premium A surcharge of ten percent added to the purchase price of auction lots.

Buy-in See *reserve.*

By-bidding See *touting.*

Call a sale To auction vocally.

Chant Calling a sale in a rhythmic monotone; a style used often by tobacco auctioneers.

Collusion An arrangement between bidders to defraud the auction house. Usually in a case of collusion two or more bidders refrain from participating in the sale so that lots can be bought cheaply.

Combine   A group of individuals organized to buy or sell a lot, usually a very expensive lot.

Commission   Amount paid to the auction gallery by the consignor or seller, usually a percentage of the sum fetched by the owner's lot or lots.

Cry (crier)   To call an auction; conduct a sale vocally.

Estimate   The projected amount, a guess by the auctioneer or cataloger, of what a lot will fetch. At Sotheby's and Christie's the lowest estimate is usually about two-thirds of the amount of the reserve.

Facsimile   An exact copy of any article, usually of much less value than the original from which it was copied.

False value   An auction value based upon items "bid in" by the consignors, so that there was actually no sale; a value established by spurious or dishonest appraisals.

Fast knockdown   See *quick knockdown.*

Fetch   To bring a certain sum at auction.

Floor bidders   Bidders present in the auction salesroom.

Gavel   See *hammer.*

Hammer   Gavel or other object held by the auctioneer with which he "knocks down" lots to successful bidders.

Hidden reserve   also known as *secret reserve.* A minimum sale price, concealed from bidders and agreed upon by the gallery and the consignor.

Ivory hammer   Pretentious term for an auctioneer's gavel.

Joint buying   See *combine.*

King of the ring   The person in charge of the ring, generally the same person who executes bids for the ring at the sale.

Kipper   See *ring.*

Knock down   To sell by the fall of the hammer.

Knock-out   Private sale of merchandise purchased at low prices (without dealer competition) by members of a ring.

Lot   Any numbered item or group of items in a sale. A lot may consist of one article or 500 articles.

Mail bid   See *order bid.*

Mark   The target for any shenanigans; a sucker; a person set up by the auction gallery for a special sale.

Misattribution   The ascription of an article to a wrong era, writer, artist, or manufacturer. A misattribution may occur by accident or with the intent to beguile bidders into paying much more or much less than the actual value of the article.

Obituaries   Death notices in the newspapers that furnish auction galleries with a source for consignments.

Off the chandelier   See *phantom bid.*

Off the wall   See *phantom bid.*

Old master   Loosely used to describe any painting executed prior to 1800 (sometimes prior to 1750 or 1700). A term used in apposition to 19th century or modern art.

On the block   See *block.*

Open sale   A sale without reserves or buy-backs; an unrestricted sale.

Order bid   A bid submitted by mail, telephone, or in person prior to the auction sale. Order bids are used competitively by the auctioneer against floor bidders at the sale.

Owned property   Lots at auction that are owned by the gallery.

Pass   To pass a lot in the sale because there is no bid, or the bid is too small or not equal to the amount of the owner's reserve.

Phantom bid   A nonexistent bid, invented by the auctioneer, to run prices up. Phantom bids are usually picked off the wall by the auctioneer, or off chandeliers, or from pillars or idle spectators in a salesroom.

Philographer (philography)   Serious collector of autograph letters and documents.

Phone bid   See *order bid.*

Plant   See *salt.*

Private treaty   Outright sale, as opposed to auction. Many auction galleries sell lots by private treaty if they do not meet their auction reserve, thus preempting the function of regular dealers.

Provenance   The pedigree or source of any lot. The older the provenance the stronger it is, as a rule; often a well-authenticated painting has a provenance that traces its ownership back several centuries. A provenance is often forged for a worthless object so that, in the final analysis, the sharp eye of an expert must take precedence over provenance.

Proxy bids   See *order bid.*

Puffing   See *touting.*

Quick knockdown   Fraudulent method of auctioneering by which the auctioneer knocks down articles so quickly that floor bidders don't have a chance to bid. Also, one or two quick knockdowns are occasionally used legitimately by an auctioneer to alert the floor bidders that they must bid quickly so the sale will proceed briskly.

Reproduction   A copy of an original, usually of much smaller value than the object copied.

Reserve   A minimum sale price agreed upon by the consignor and the auction house beneath which the lot will not be sold. If the lot does not meet or exceed the reserve, the property is usually returned to the consignor with a bill for five percent of the last legitimate bid on the lot. Reserves are also known as bid-ins, buy-ins, or stop-prices.

Ring   A group of cheats formed to defraud the auction gallery by having one or more of their members execute bids for the entire group. The ring, or kipper, is designed to eliminate all dealer competition at a sale. The lots purchased cheaply are later auctioned in a private "knock-out" held by the ring.

Running, or **trotting** The illegal technique of forcing bidding up by taking bids off the wall, off the chandelier, or from a shill. (A "single trot" is when the auctioneer pits a phantom bidder against a live bidder; a "double trot" is when the auctioneer has no live bidder and works the bids up with two phantom bidders.)

Salt, or **plant** To pad a "name" sale with inferior items from other sources, usually consigned by dealers.

Secret reserve A minimum sale price, or reserve, that is agreed upon between the gallery and the consignor and is concealed from bidders. See also *reserve*.

Sharpshoot To watch the bidding with a cunning eye and bid on any significant lot that's about to sell for less than its value; to pick off the choice items at a sale.

Shill A phony bidder who works with the auctioneer to "run" bidders.

Shutout bid A huge jump in the bidding, double or triple the bid necessary, in order to bluff out all competition. Often the shutout bid represents the bidder's limit.

Sleeper An article of which the importance or high value is not known to the seller.

Sold to the order See *order bid.*

Stop price See *reserve.*

Switch A dishonest maneuver by which one item is exchanged for another of lesser value. The switch may occur before or after a sale.

Telephone bid See *order bid.*

Tie bid When two persons bid the same amount simultaneously. If one bid is a mail bid, then the mail bid (since it was received earlier) takes priority over the floor bid. If both bids are on the floor, the successful bid is usually that of the bidder closer to the auctioneer.

Touting, or **puffing** Loudly praising the merchandise offered at auction, either before or during the sale, by an agent of the auctioneer. Such as: "What a beautiful painting! I think it's a Corot." A touter or puffer may also act as an auctioneer's shill.

Trotting See *running*.

Under the hammer See *hammer*.

Unrestricted sale A sale without reserves or buy-backs; an open sale.

Up for grabs Up for sale at auction.

Upset price See *reserve*.

Withdraw Remove a lot from auction because of misattribution, questioned ownership or authenticity, or any other valid reason.

Index